ACCESS

Fundamentals of Literacy and Communication

Steven J. Molinsky
Bill Bliss

Contributing Authors

Carol H. Van Duzer
Elizabeth M. Bailey

PRENTICE HALL REGENTS, Englewood Cliffs, New Jersey 07632

Library of Congress Cataloging-in-Publication Data

Molinsky, Steven J.
  Access: Fundamentals of literacy and communication /
Steven J. Molinsky, Bill Bliss; contributing authors, Carol H.
Van Duzer, Elizabeth M. Bailey.
     p. 128
     ISBN 0-13-004235-8
     1. English language—Textbooks for foreign speakers.
I. Bliss, Bill. II. Van Duzer, Carol H. III. Bailey, Elizabeth M.
IV. Title
PE1128.M67   1988
428.2'4—dc20   90-31801
                                                    CIP

Editorial/production supervision
 and interior design: Noël Vreeland Carter
Cover design: Karen Stephens
Manufacturing buyer: Ray Keating

Illustrations by Gabriel Polonsky and Don Martinetti

TO THE TEACHER

The **ACCESS Teacher's Guide** should be used in conjunction with this text. The guide contains essential communication activities designed to accompany the lessons in this student book. It also offers strategies for developing basic literacy and numeracy concepts, and comprehensive lesson plans for the critically important first weeks of instruction in literacy and communication.

© 1990 by Prentice Hall Regents

Printed in the United States of America

20   19   18   17   16

ISBN 0-13-004235-8

CONTENTS

PART ONE

Reading Readiness Skills

PART TWO

Writing Readiness Skills

PART THREE

Literacy and Communication

Letter Recognition • Word Recognition • Alphabet
• Upper Case Letters • Lower Case Letters
• Personal Information: Name, Family Members

Counting • Number Recognition • Numbers: 1-20
• Personal Information: Age, Address, Telephone

Streets • Place Names • Street Names
• Counting and Writing Numbers: 1-100
• Bus Route Information

APPENDIX

READING READINESS SKILLS

PART ONE

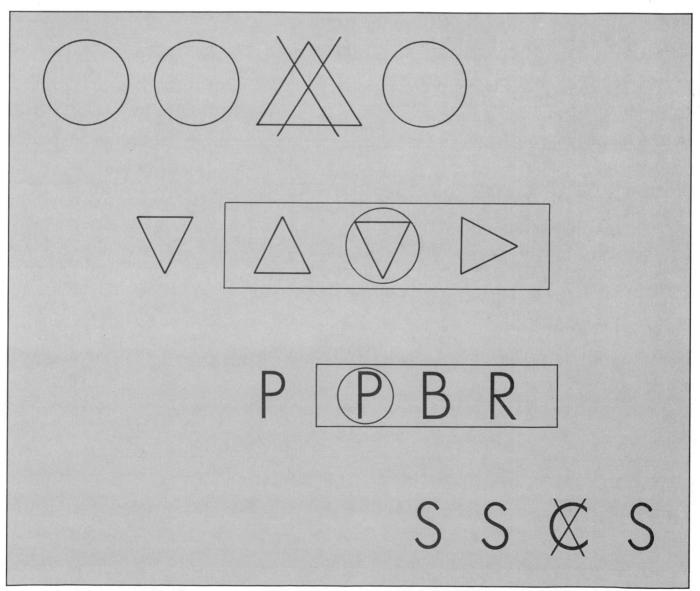

PUT AN X ON THE DIFFERENT SHAPE.

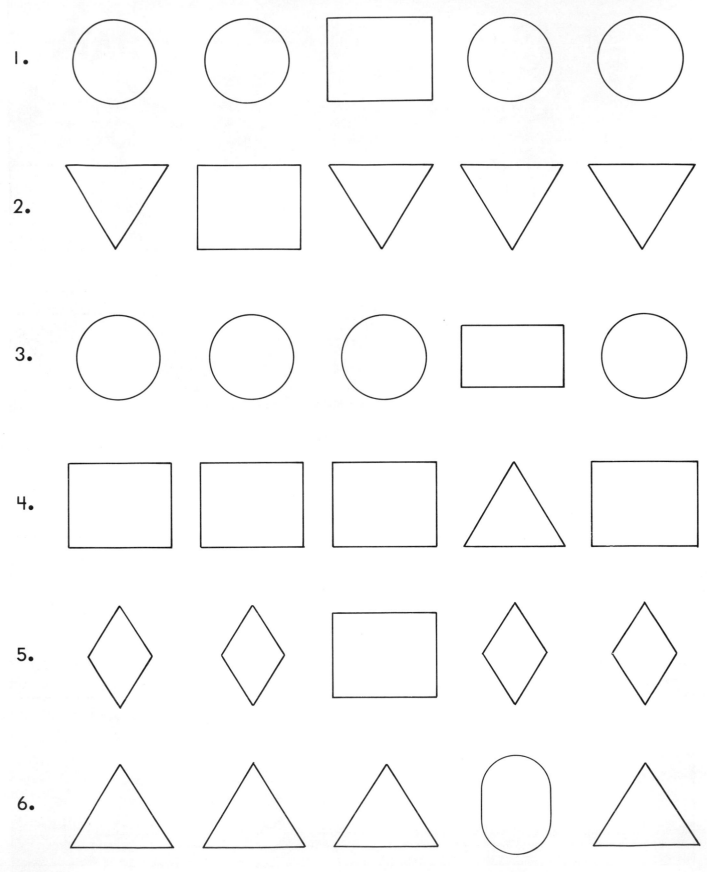

1.

2.

3.

4.

5.

6.

2

PUT AN X ON THE DIFFERENT SHAPE.

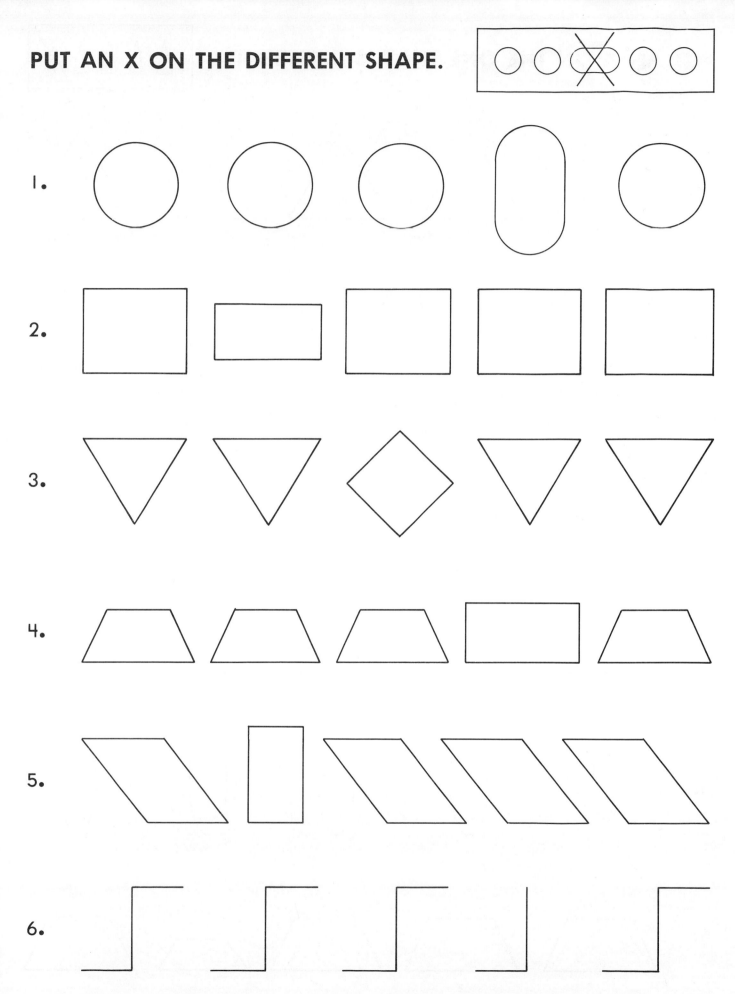

3

PUT AN X ON THE ONE THAT IS DIFFERENT.

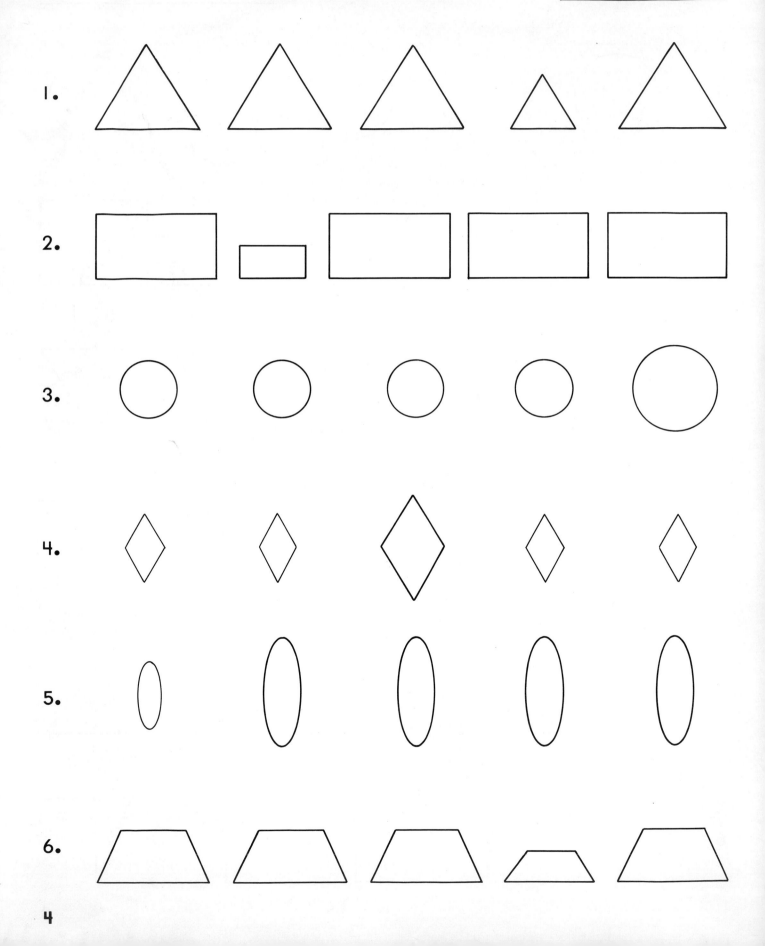

1.

2.

3.

4.

5.

6.

PUT AN X ON THE ONE THAT IS DIFFERENT.

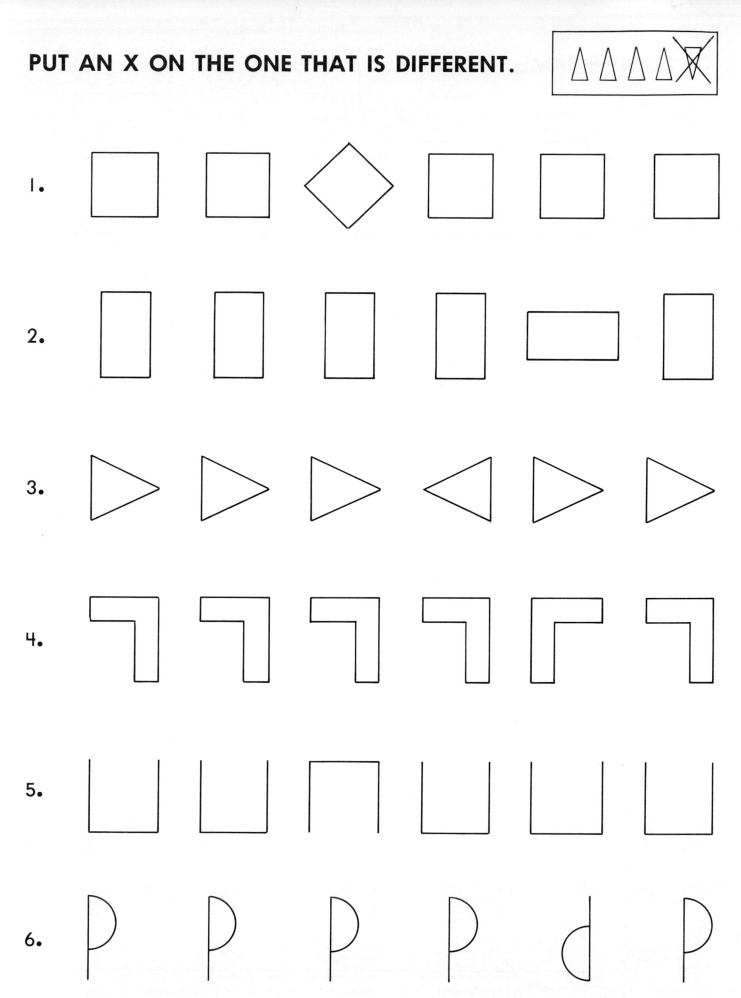

1.

2.

3.

4.

5.

6.

5

CIRCLE THE SAME SHAPE.

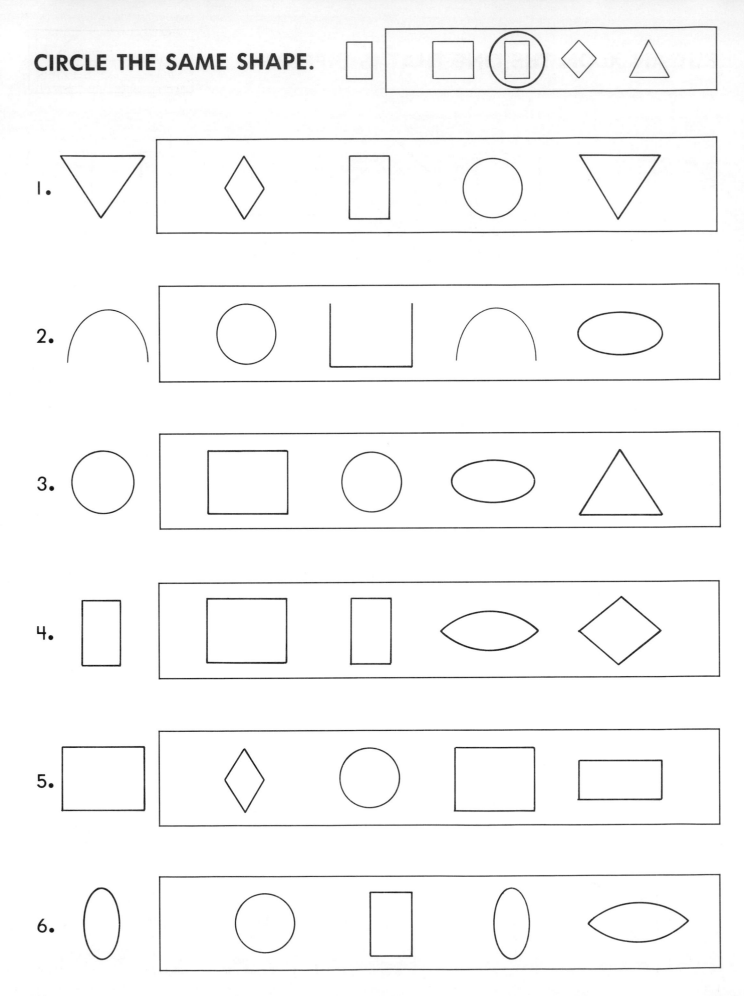

CIRCLE THE SAME SHAPE.

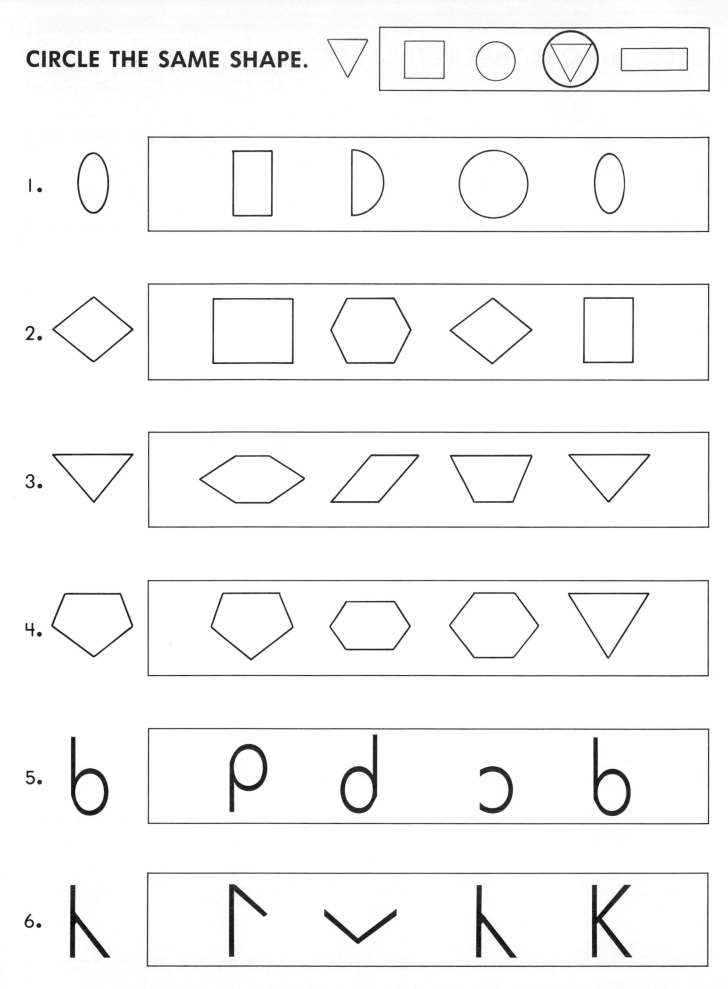

CIRCLE THE ONE THAT IS THE SAME.

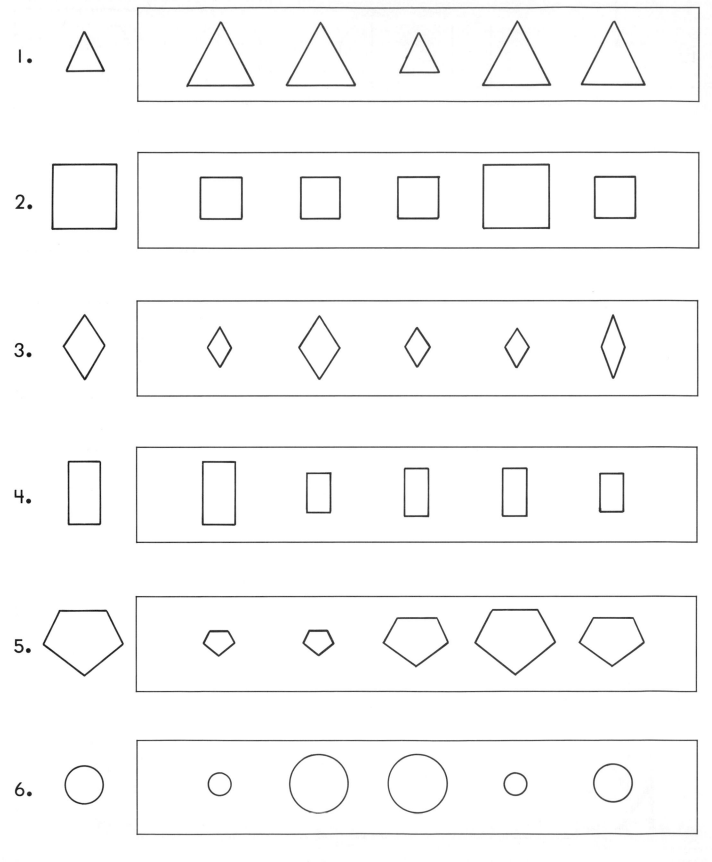

1.

2.

3.

4.

5.

6.

8

CIRCLE THE ONE THAT IS THE SAME.

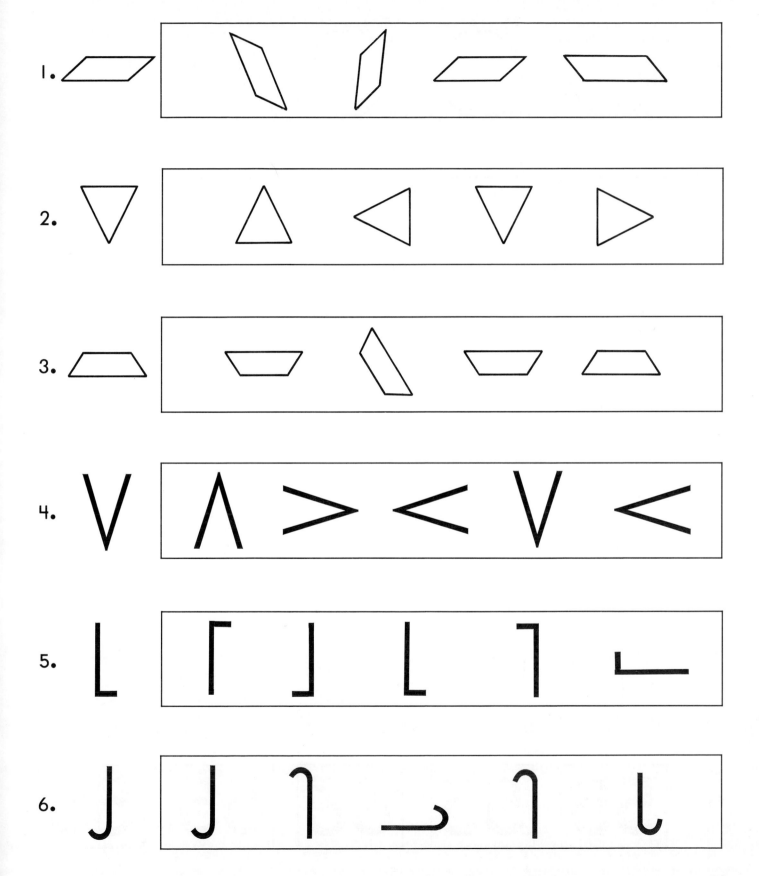

PUT AN X ON THE ONE THAT IS DIFFERENT.

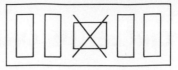

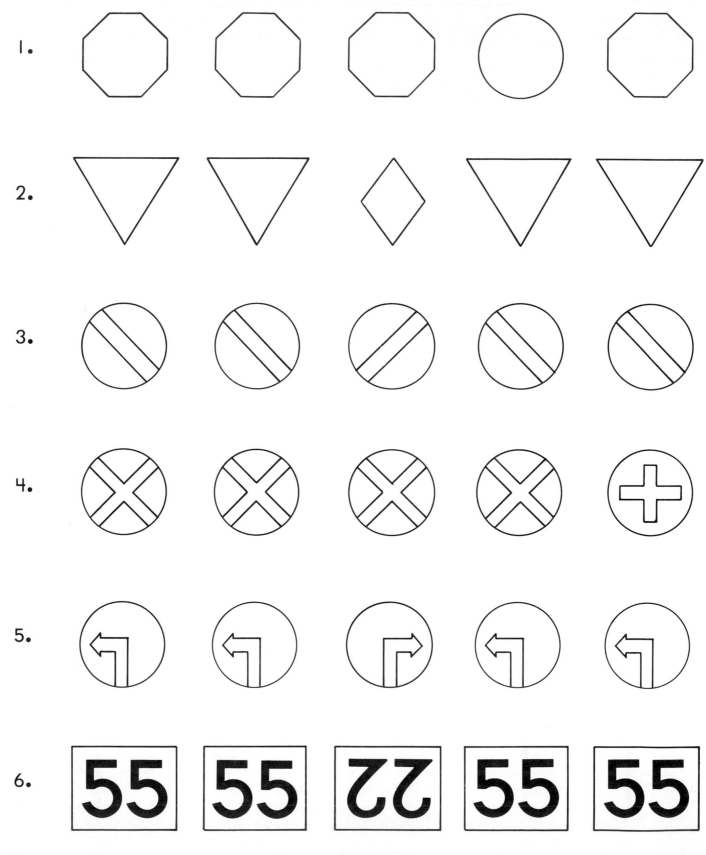

1.

2.

3.

4.

5.

6.

10

PUT AN X ON THE DIFFERENT LETTER.

T T T̸X̸ T T

1. T T T S T T

2. C C C V C C

3. I I G I I I

4. A J A A A A

5. O O N O O O

6. Z U Z Z Z Z

PUT AN X ON THE DIFFERENT LETTER.

1. V V A V V V V

2. F F F F F E F

3. W W W M W W W

4. O O O O Q O O

5. T I T T T T T

6. P P P R P P

12

CIRCLE THE SAME LETTERS.

P P B P R D P

1. F | H V F A G F

2. J | J L K C J J

3. S | U M C S T S

4. B | B Z B O A B

5. Y | M Y L Y P E

6. R | R N R B P R

CIRCLE THE SAME LETTERS. F T (F) E K (F) (F)

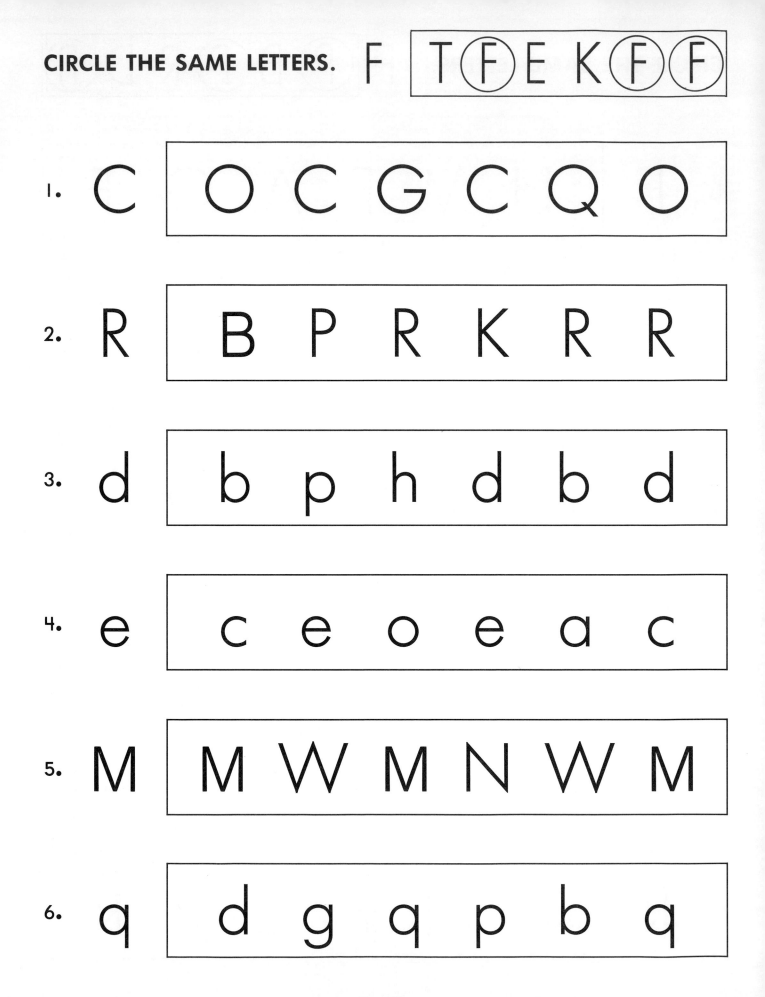

1. C   O C G C Q O

2. R   B P R K R R

3. d   b p h d b d

4. e   c e o e a c

5. M   M W M N W M

6. q   d g q p b q

14

PUT AN X ON THE DIFFERENT LETTER.

| S | S | C̸ | S | S |

1. L L L L A L L

2. E E E E J E E

3. Y Y Y Y V Y Y

4. W W W W W M W

5. P P P P R P P

6. T T T T I T T

7. O O O Q O O O

8. p p p q p p p

9. d d b d d d d

10. h h n h h h h

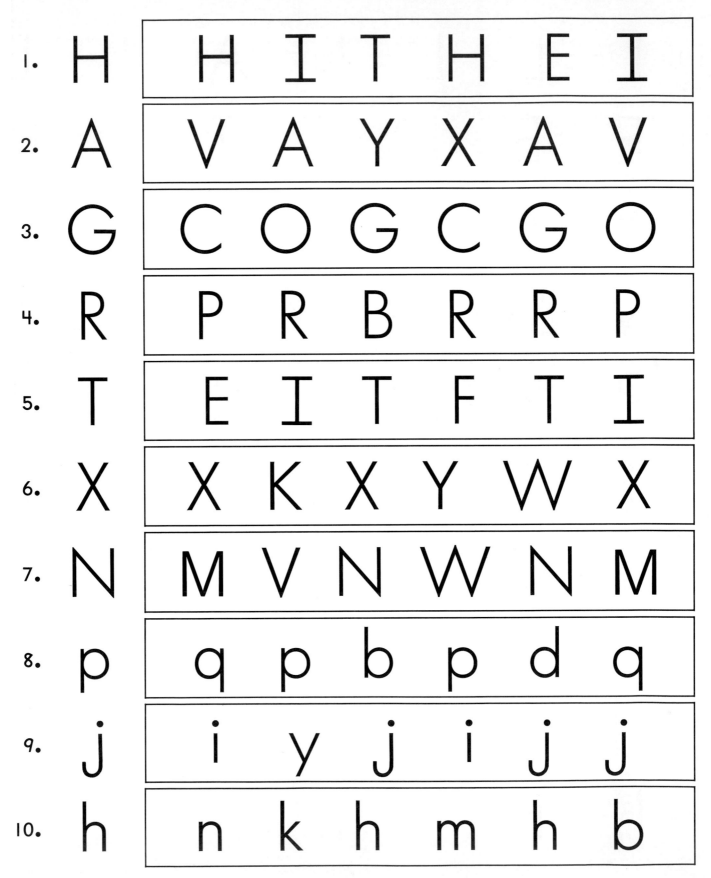

1. H   H I T H E I
2. A   V A Y X A V
3. G   C O G C G O
4. R   P R B R R P
5. T   E I T F T I
6. X   X K X Y W X
7. N   M V N W N M
8. p   q p b p d q
9. j   i y j i j j
10. h   n k h m h b

16

WRITING READINESS SKILLS

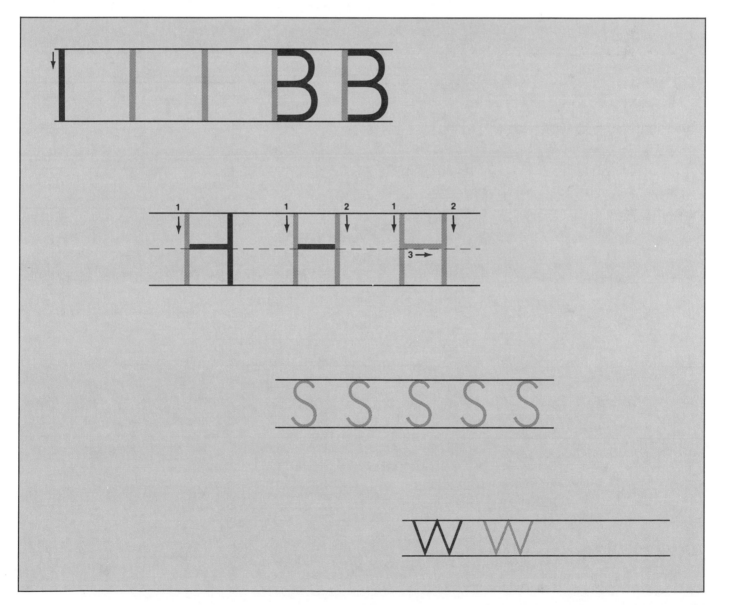

PART TWO

STARTING STROKES

TRACE.

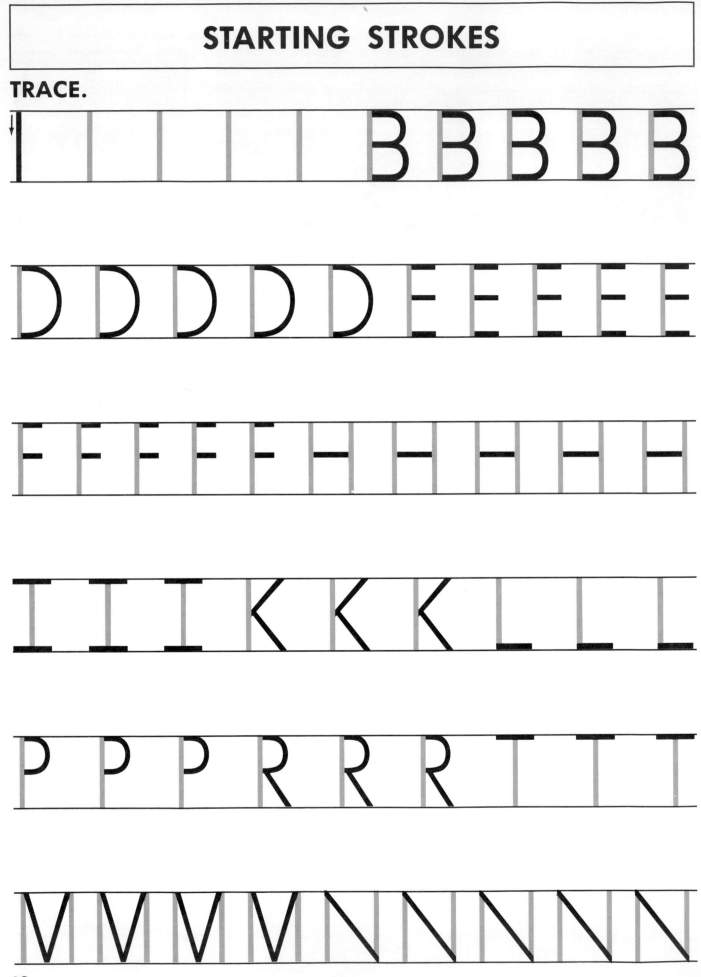

TRACE.

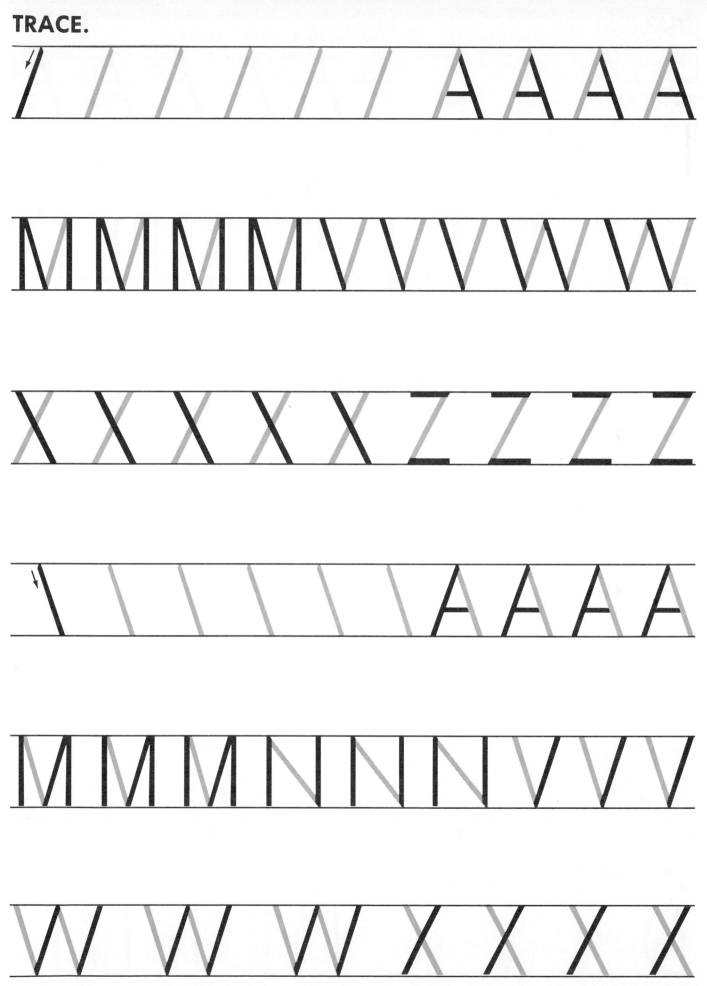

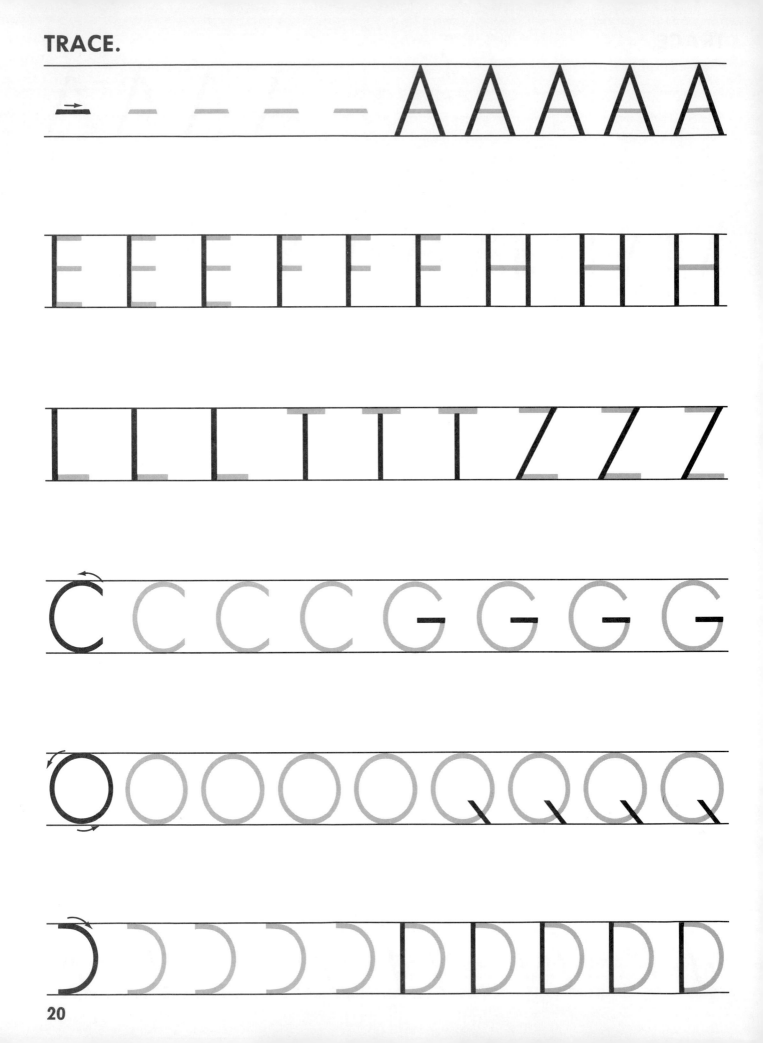

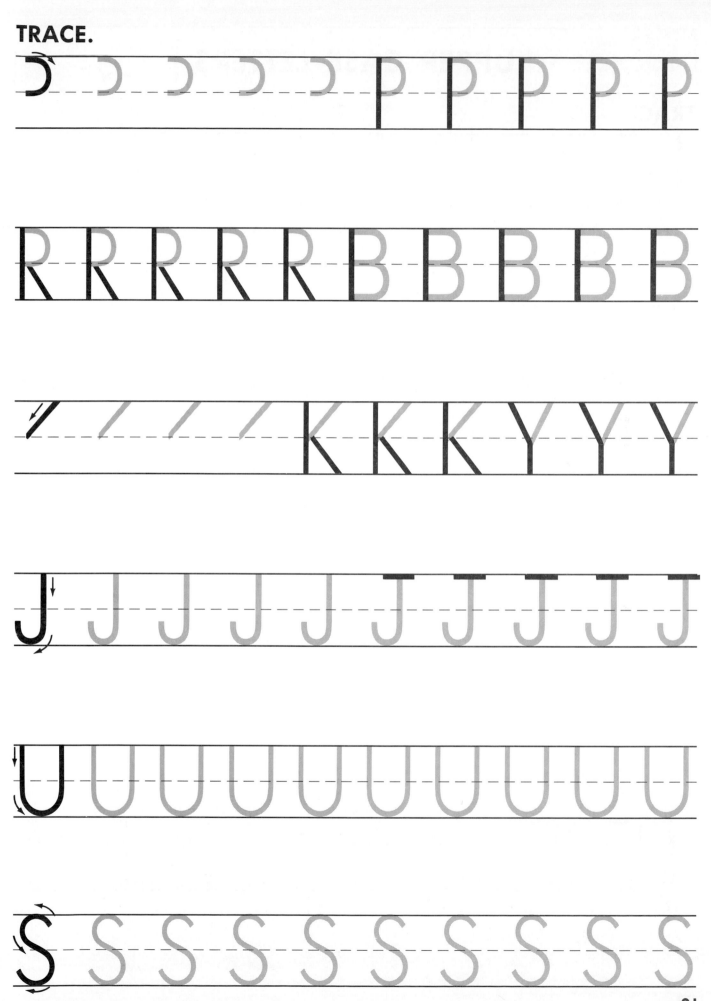

UPPER CASE LETTERS

TRACE.

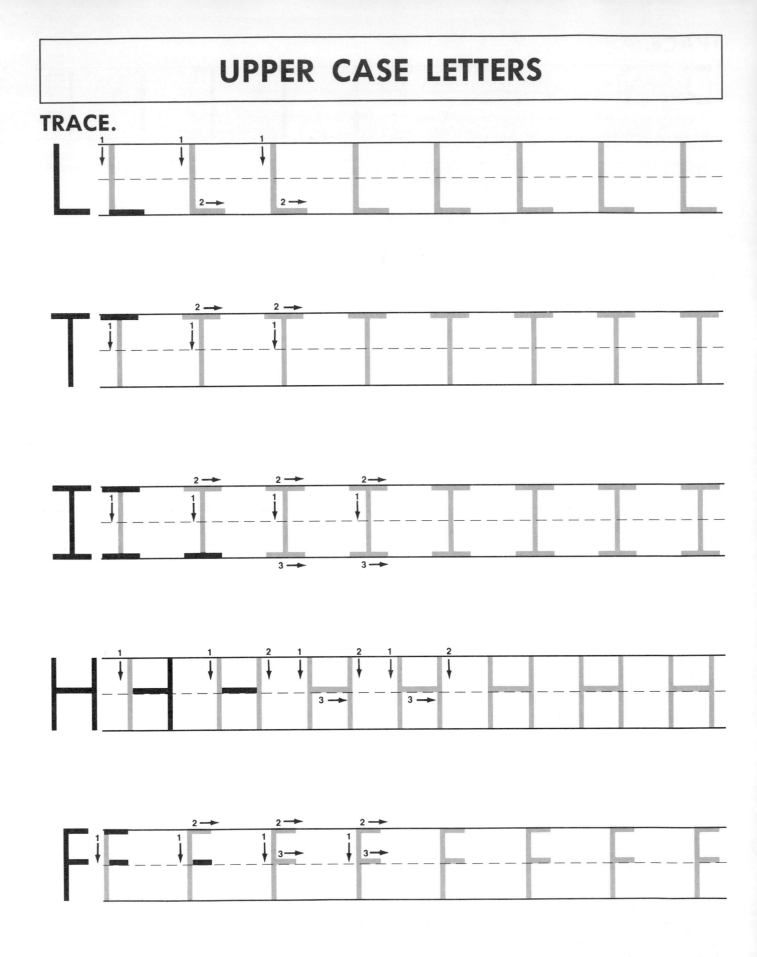

TRACE AND COPY.

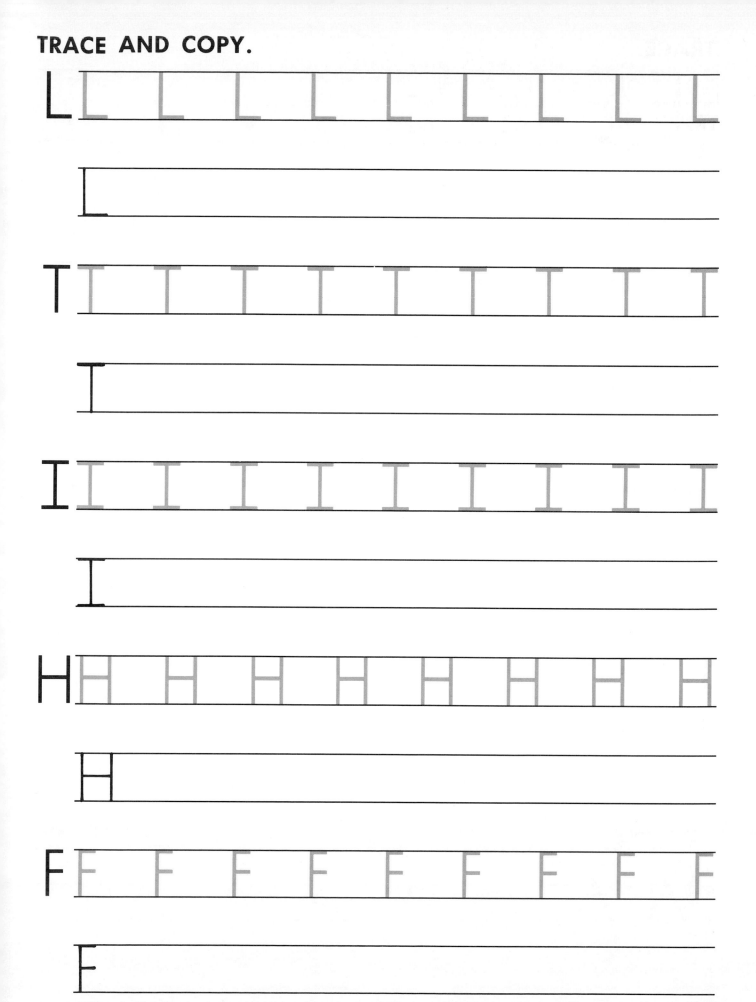

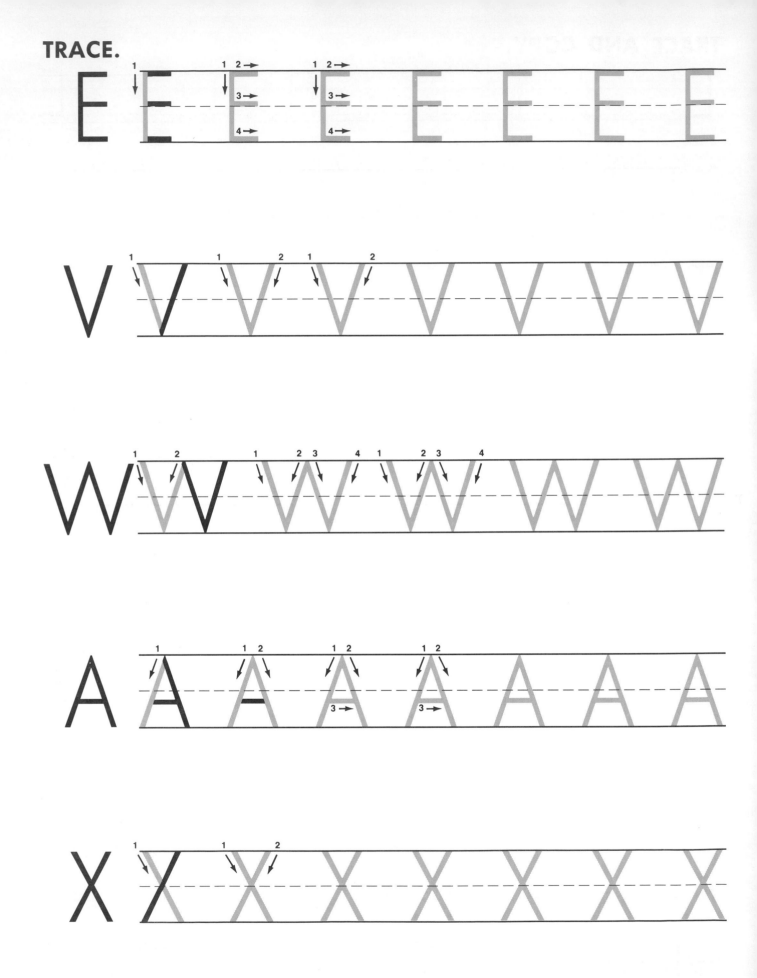

TRACE AND COPY.

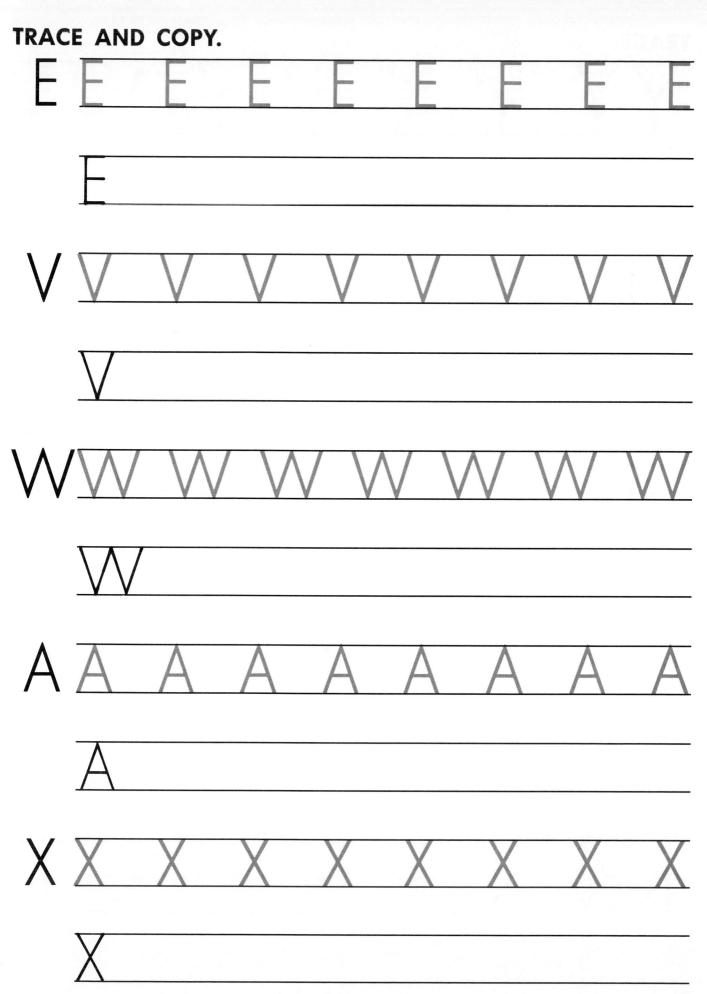

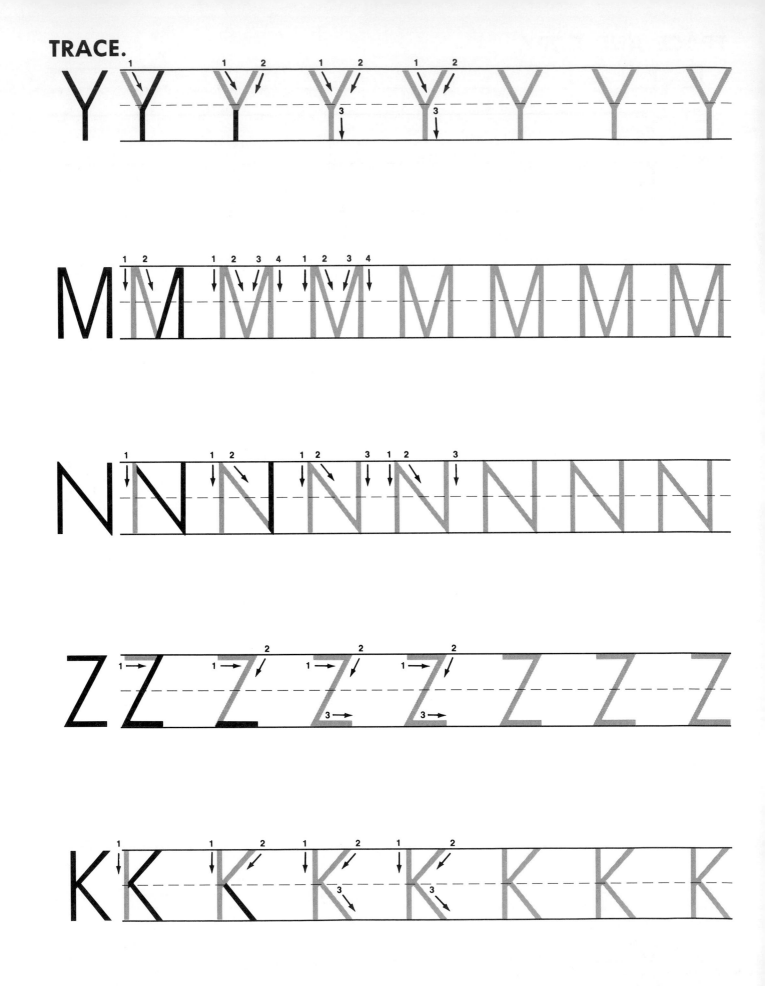

TRACE AND COPY.

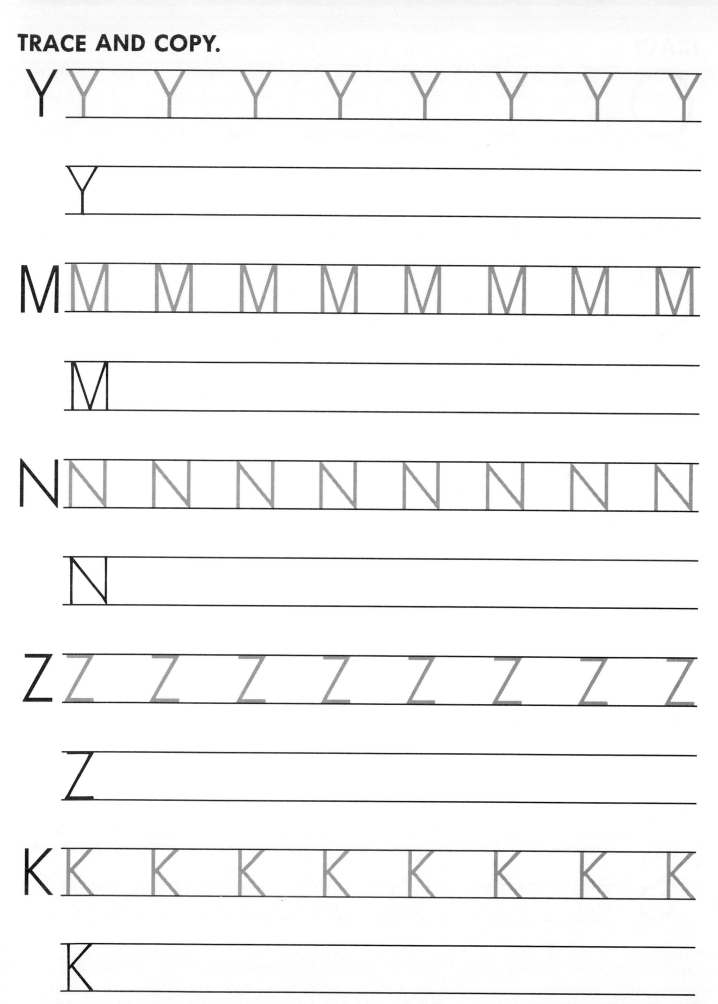

TRACE.

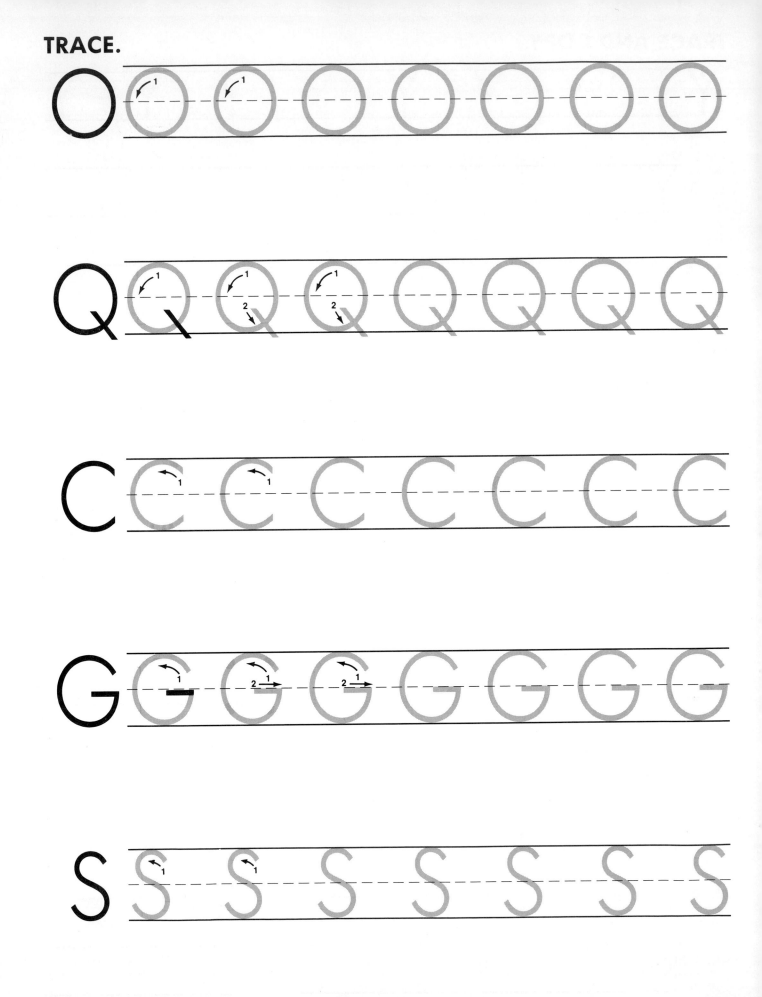

TRACE AND COPY.

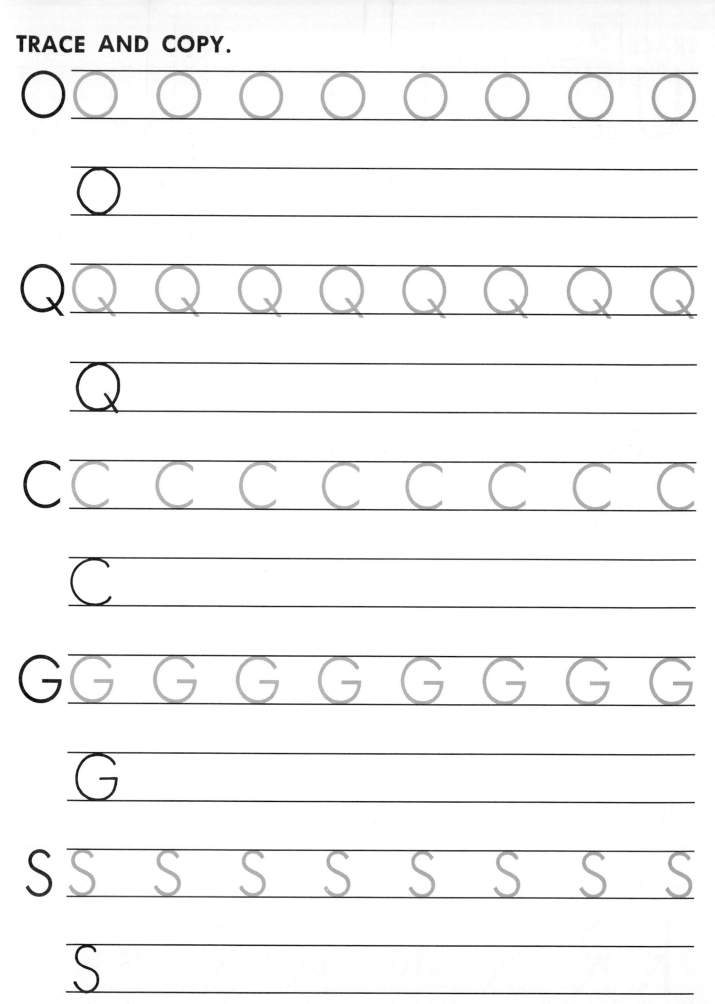

O O O O O O O O O

O

Q Q Q Q Q Q Q Q Q

Q

C C C C C C C C C

C

G G G G G G G G G

G

S S S S S S S S S

S

TRACE.

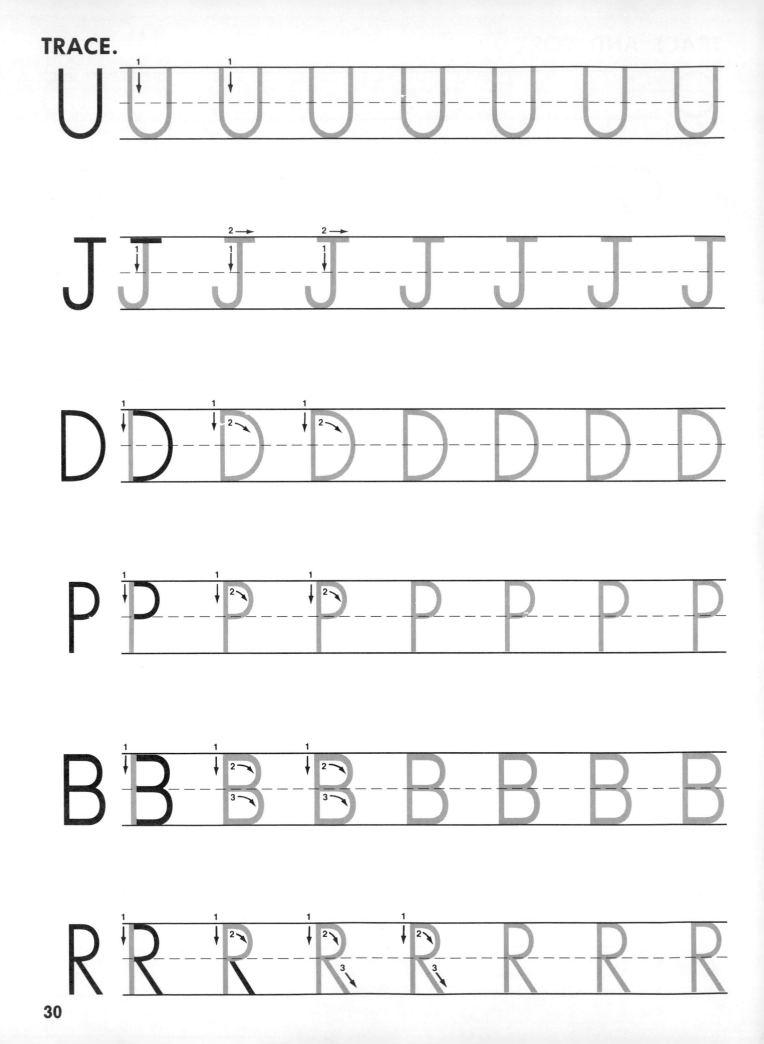

TRACE AND COPY.

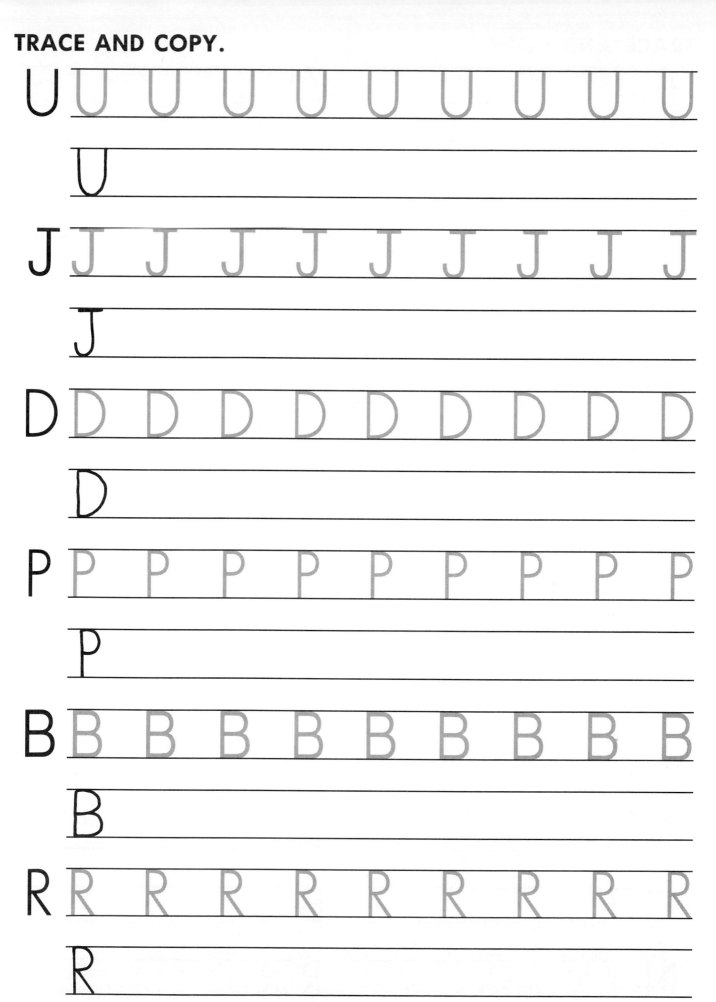

U U U U U U U U U U U

U

J J J J J J J J J J J J

J

D D D D D D D D D D

D

P P P P P P P P P P

P

B B B B B B B B B B

B

R R R R R R R R R R R

R

TRACE AND COPY.

L L _____   Z Z _____

T T _____   K K _____

I I _____   O O _____

H H _____   Q Q _____

F F _____   C C _____

E E _____   G G _____

V V _____   S S _____

W W _____   U U _____

A A _____   J J _____

X X _____   D D _____

Y Y _____   P P _____

M M _____   B B _____

N N _____   R R _____

LITERACY AND COMMUNICATION

PART THREE

NAMES

NUMBERS

PLACES

TIME

HEALTH

MONEY

JOBS

SIGNS

FRIENDS

NAMES

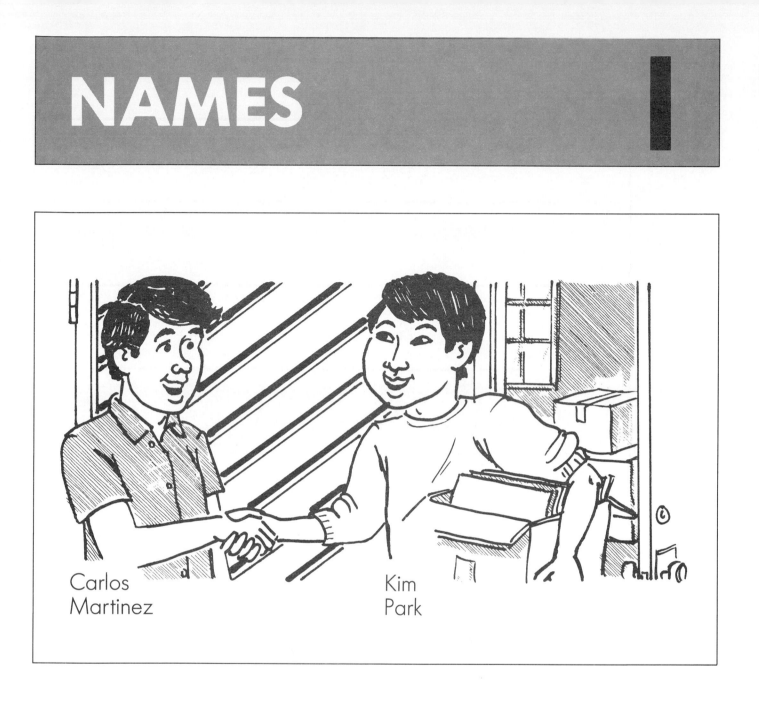

Carlos
Martinez

Kim
Park

Sue
Smith

Jane
Johnson

Tom
Jones

Karen
Wilson

Mary
Warner

Bob
Lee

1.

2.

3.

CIRCLE THE SAME LETTER.

1. C	O	Ⓒ	Q	D
2. L	L	T	F	U
3. M	N	H	M	W
4. Y	V	W	Y	X
5. P	B	P	D	F
6. j	q	i	J	l
7. t	t	l	i	f
8. e	c	u	o	e
9. r	n	v	r	m
10. b	p	h	d	b

36

CIRCLE THE SAME WORD.

1. NAME	MAN	(NAME)	MEN	MEAN
2. NAME	MEAN	MANE	MAN	NAME
3. Name	Neat	Mean	Name	Mane
4. LAST	LIST	LASH	STAY	LAST
5. last	lash	least	last	list

WRITE YOUR LAST NAME.

1. LAST NAME _____

2. _____
LAST NAME

3. Name _____
Last

4.

Last name

1. CLAYTON

2. BRENNER

3. KWAN

4. KELTON

CIRCLE THE SAME WORD.

1. FIRST	FIST	FINE	(FIRST)	FLIT
2. FIRST	FIRST	FLIRT	STIR	FIR
3. first	flirt	fist	frost	first
4. LAST	LATE	LEAST	LAST	LIST
5. Last	Less	Last	Lame	Lash

WRITE YOUR NAME.

1. _____

  FIRST NAME   LAST NAME

2. NAME _____

       FIRST   LAST

3. [   ]

First name   Last name

4. _____

  LAST NAME   FIRST NAME

5. _____

  Name: First   Last

TRACE AND COPY THE ALPHABET.

A A _____   N N _____

B B _____   O O _____

C C _____   P P _____

D D _____   Q Q _____

E E _____   R R _____

F F _____   S S _____

G G _____   T T _____

H H _____   U U _____

I I _____   V V _____

J J _____   W W _____

K K _____   X X _____

L L _____   Y Y _____

M M _____   Z Z _____

FILL IN THE MISSING LETTERS.

1. A B C̲ D E F G ___ I

J K ___ M N ___ P Q R

___ T U V ___ X Y Z

2. A ___ C D ___ F G H ___

J ___ L M ___ O P Q ___

S T ___ V W X ___ Z

WRITE THE ALPHABET.

A̲ ___ ___ ___ ___ ___

___ ___ ___ ___ ___ ___

___ ___ ___ ___ ___ ___

___ ___ ___ ___ ___ ___

41

LOWER CASE LETTERS

TRACE.

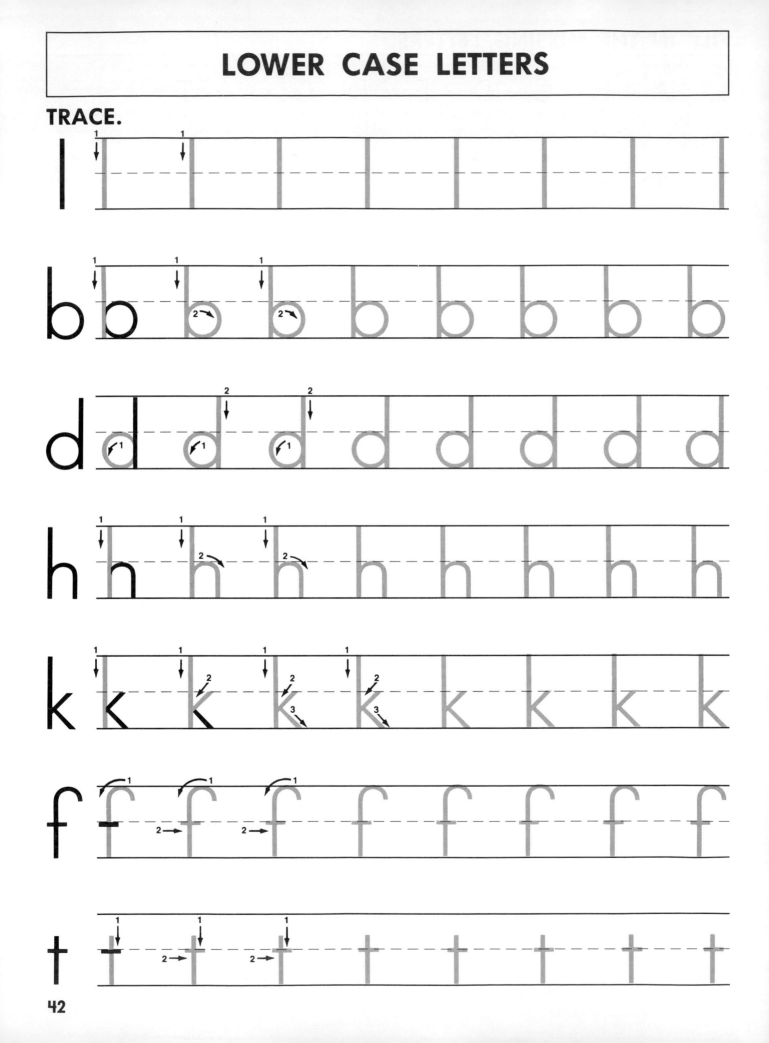

TRACE AND COPY.

l

b b b b b b b b b
b

d d d d d d d d d
d

h h h h h h h h h
h

k k k k k k k k k
k

f f f f f f f f f
f

t t t t t t t t t
t

43

TRACE.

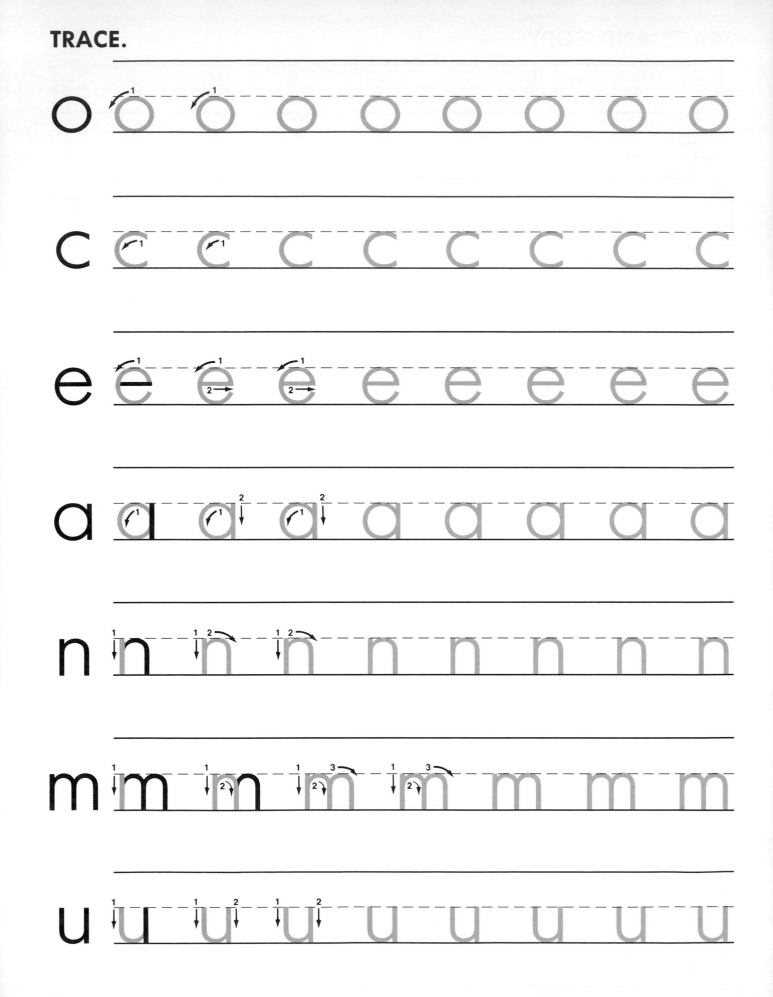

TRACE AND COPY.

o o o o o o o o o o

o

c c c c c c c c c c

c

e e e e e e e e e e

e

a a a a a a a a a a

a

n n n n n n n n n n

n

m m m m m m m m m m

m

u u u u u u u u u u

u

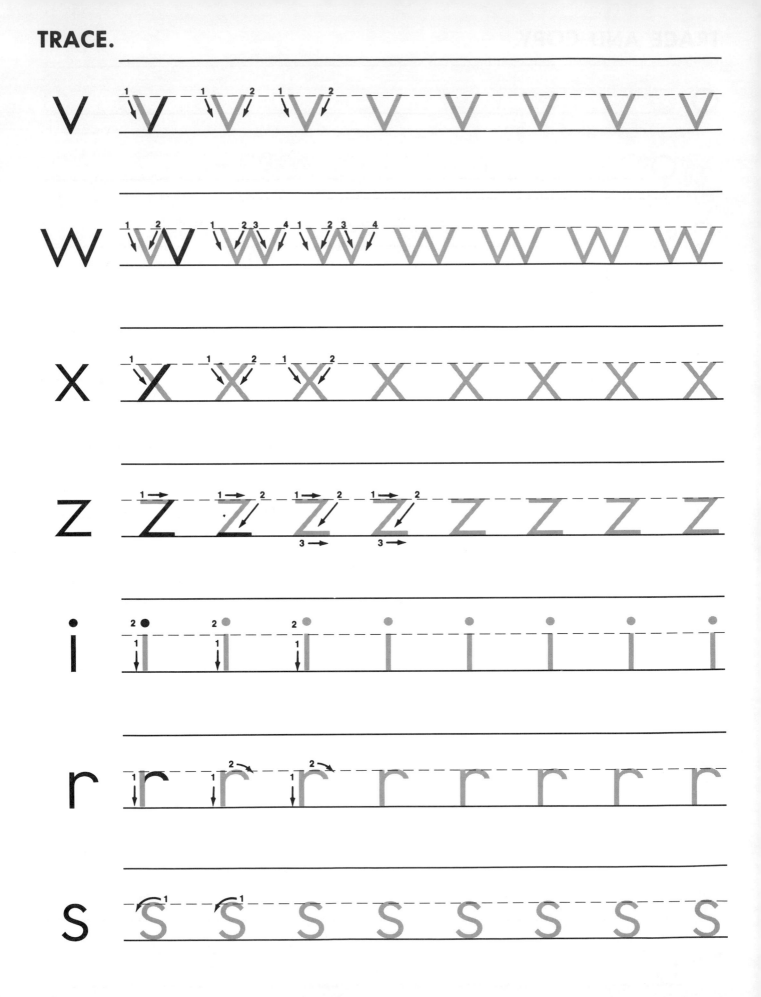

TRACE AND COPY.

V   V V V V V V V V V V

V

W   W W W W W W W W

W

X   X X X X X X X X X

X

z   z z z z z z z z z

z

i   i i i i i i i i i

i

r   r r r r r r r r r

r

s   s s s s s s s s s

s

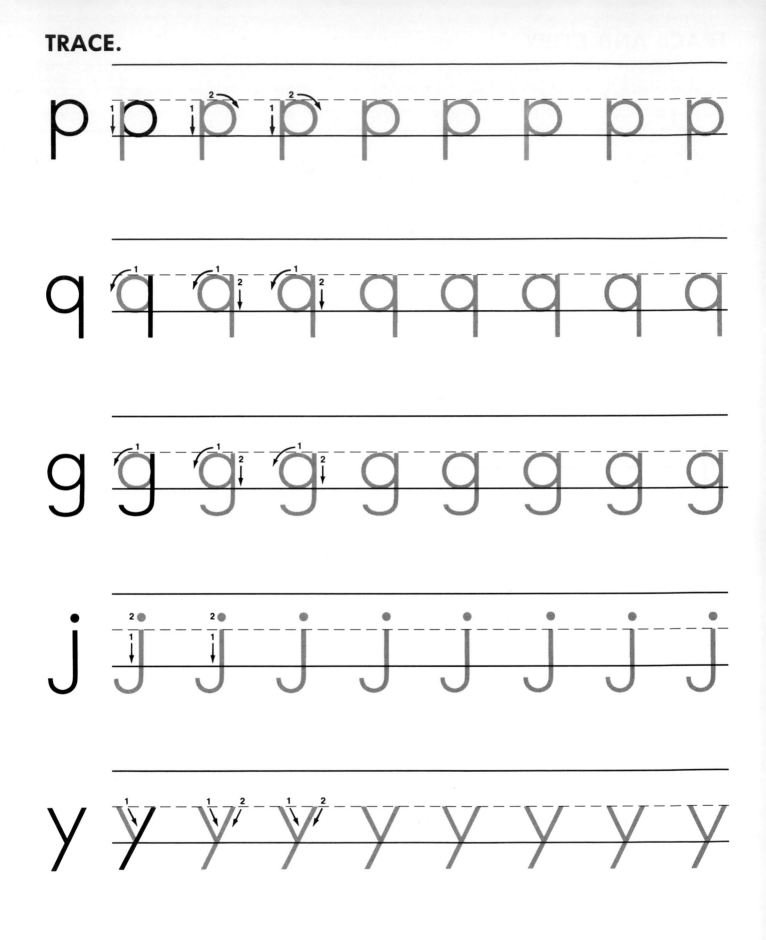

TRACE AND COPY.

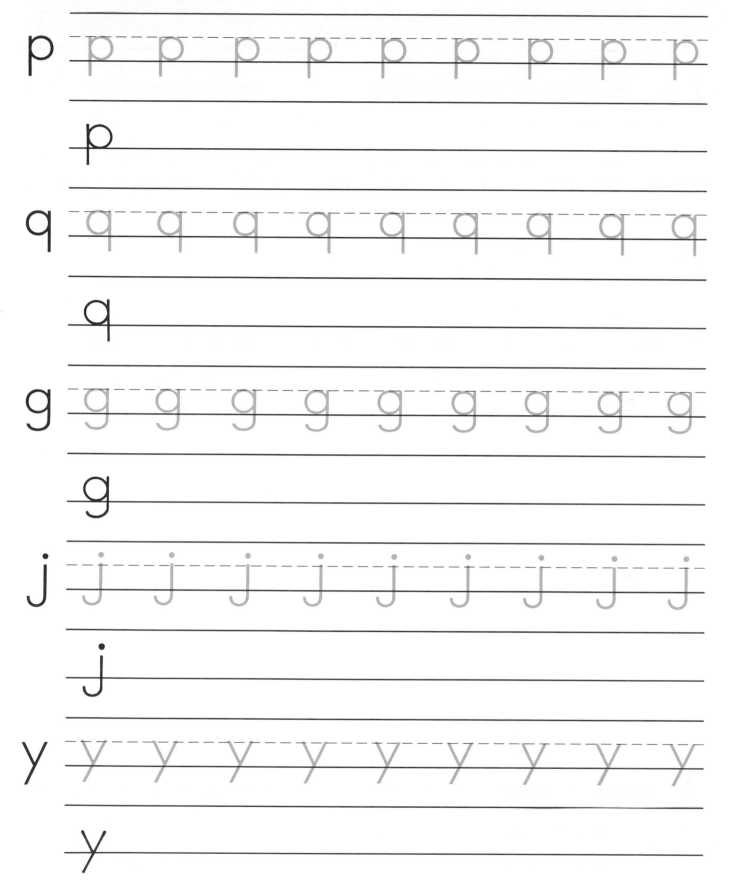

p p p p p p p p p p

p

q q q q q q q q q q

q

g g g g g g g g g g

g

j j j j j j j j j

j

y y y y y y y y y y

y

TRACE AND COPY THE ALPHABET.

a a   n n

b b   o o

c c   p p

d d   q q

e e   r r

f f   s s

g g   t t

h h   u u

i i   v v

j j   w w

k k   x x

l l   y y

m m   z z

TRACE AND COPY THE ALPHABET.

Aa   Aa   Aa

Bb   Bb   Bb

Cc   Cc   Cc

Dd   Dd   Dd

Ee   Ee   Ee

Ff   Ff   Ff

Gg   Gg   Gg

Hh   Hh   Hh

Ii   Ii   Ii

Jj   Jj   Jj

Kk   Kk   Kk

Ll   Ll   Ll

Mm   Mm   Mm

TRACE AND COPY THE ALPHABET.

Nn   Nn Nn _____

Oo   Oo Oo _____

Pp   Pp Pp _____

Qq   Qq Qq _____

Rr   Rr Rr _____

Ss   Ss Ss _____

Tt   Tt Tt _____

Uu   Uu Uu _____

Vv   Vv Vv _____

Ww   Ww Ww _____

Xx   Xx Xx _____

Yy   Yy Yy _____

Zz   Zz Zz _____

MATCH THE LETTERS. DRAW A LINE.

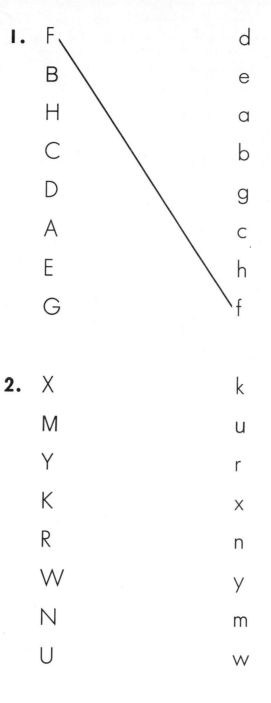

1. F   d

  B   e

  H   a

  C   b

  D   g

  A   c

  E   h

  G   f

2. X   k

  M   u

  Y   r

  K   x

  R   n

  W   y

  N   m

  U   w

WRITE THE ALPHABET.

a _____ _____ _____ _____ _____ _____

_____ _____ _____ _____ _____ _____ _____

_____ _____ _____ _____ _____ _____ _____

_____ _____ _____ _____ _____ _____ _____

🎬 LISTEN AND CIRCLE THE LETTERS YOU HEAR.

1.	AX	AF	(AS)
2.	FE	ME	NE
3.	SIR	FIR	NIR
4.	DOM	BOM	TOM
5.	JOAN	JOIN	JOUN
6.	list	lost	last
7.	name	lame	mame
8.	flirt	first	fixed
9.	Karen	Karin	Karon
10.	Blanto	Blaneo	Blanco

🎬 LISTEN AND WRITE THE NAMES YOU HEAR.

1. _____ Kim _____

2. _____

3. _____

4. _____

5. _____

6. _____

7. _____

8. _____

9. _____

10. _____

54

INTERVIEW FIVE PEOPLE.

What's your first name?

How do you spell it?

What's your last name?

How do you spell it?

1. NAME _____
        FIRST   LAST

2. NAME _____
        FIRST   LAST

3. NAME _____
        FIRST   LAST

4. _____
   First   Last

5. Name _____
        first   last

SPEAKING PRACTICE

husband
Michael

1. wife
Jane

2. father
Mr. Lopez

3. mother
Mrs. Wong

4. son
Tom

5. daughter
Ann

CIRCLE THE SAME WORD.

1. MOTHER	FATHER	(MOTHER)	BROTHER
2. WIFE	WINE	WAIT	WIFE
3. SON	SUN	SON	SO
4. FATHER	FATHER	FATTER	FASTER
5. husband	houseman	husband	happened
6. daughter	brother	laughter	daughter

MATCH THE WORDS. DRAW A LINE.

1.	NAME	mother
2.	FIRST	wife
3.	LAST	husband
4.	WIFE	name
5.	SON	father
6.	MOTHER	last
7.	FATHER	son
8.	HUSBAND	first

1.   X   ___   2.   ___   ___

3.   ___   ___   4.   ___   ___

5.   ___   ___   6.   ___   ___

NUMBERS

1 2 3 4 5 6 7 8 9 10

David
6

Maria
10

1. Franco
8

2. Ann
5

3. Lee
4

COUNT.

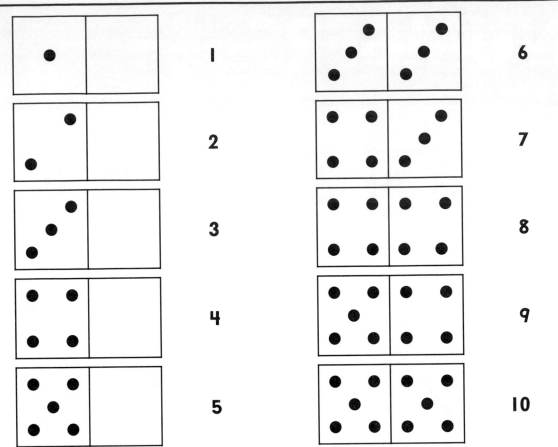

1

2

3

4

5

6

7

8

9

10

DRAW A LINE.

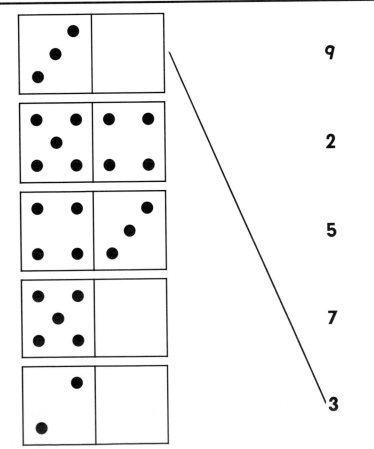

9

2

5

7

3

60

PUT AN X ON THE DIFFERENT NUMBER.

1. 6   6   6   X   6   6   6

2. 4   4   7   4   4   4   4

3. 5   5   5   5   5   2   5

4. 1   7   1   1   1   1   1

5. 9   9   9   9   6   9   9

6. 8   8   8   8   8   8   3

CIRCLE THE SAME NUMBERS.

1.	3	8	③	③	9
2.	1	7	1	9	1
3.	4	4	9	4	5
4.	6	6	9	1	6
5.	8	3	8	9	8
6.	7	1	9	1	7
7.	10	1	9	10	6
8.	2	5	2	9	5

NUMBERS

TRACE.

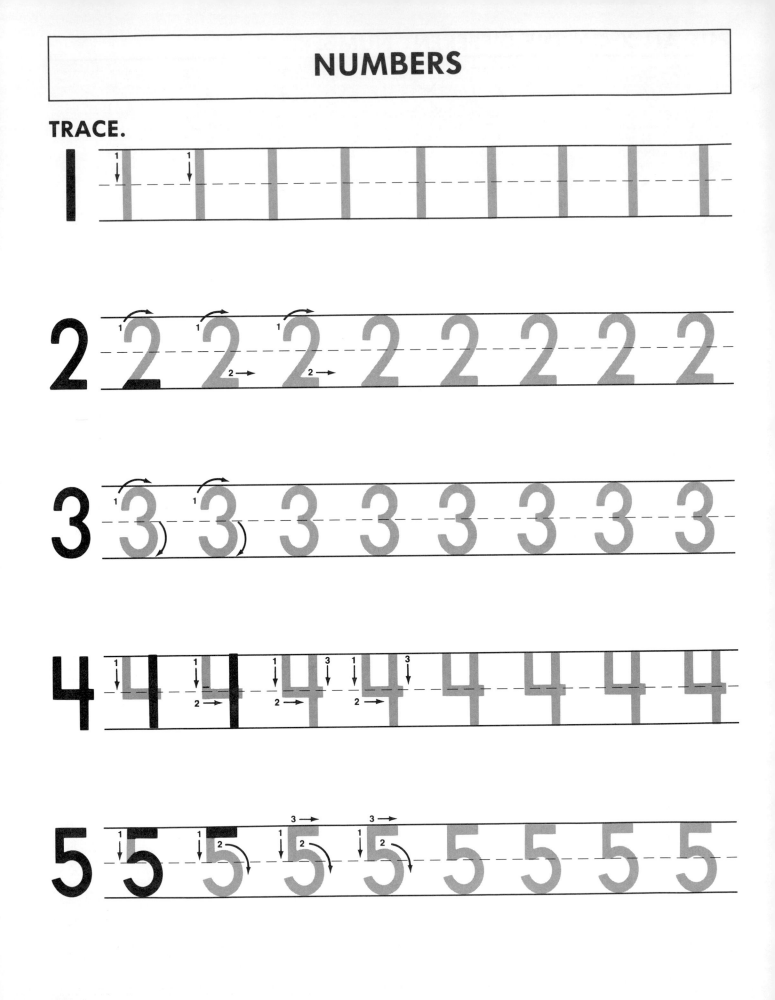

TRACE AND COPY.

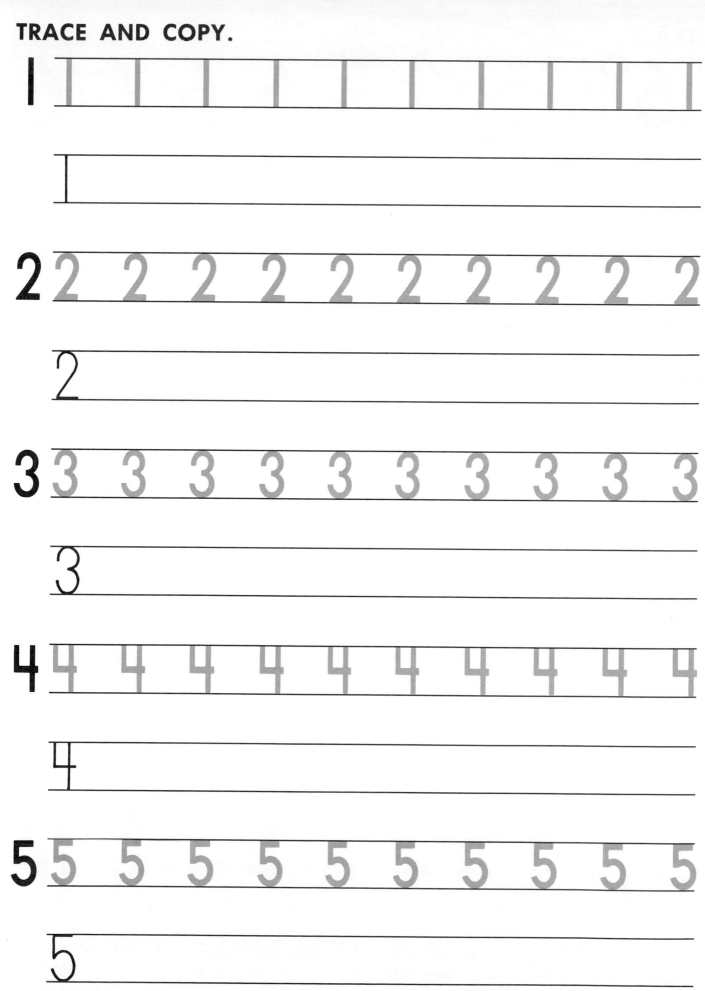

6 6 6 6 6 6 6 6 6

7 7 7 7 7 7 7 7 7

8 8 8 8 8 8 8 8 8

9 9 9 9 9 9 9 9 9

10 10 10 10 10 10 10

TRACE AND COPY.

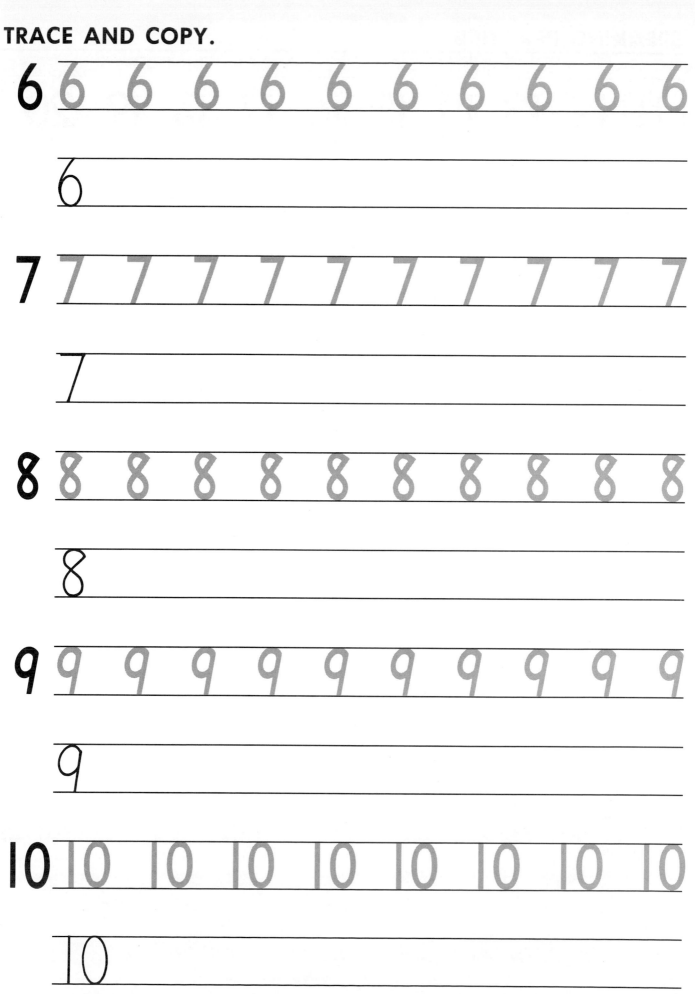

11 12 13 14 15 16 17 18 19 20

1.

2.

3.

4.

CIRCLE THE SAME NUMBER.

1.	15	(15)	5	6	16
2.	19	1	91	19	61
3.	13	3	18	31	13
4.	5	6	5	15	7
5.	20	10	2	22	20
6.	12	2	22	12	21
7.	16	16	19	61	91
8.	11	10	11	17	71

TRACE AND COPY THE NUMBERS.

11 11 __ __ __   16 16 __ __ __

12 12 __ __ __   17 17 __ __ __

13 13 __ __ __   18 18 __ __ __

14 14 __ __ __   19 19 __ __ __

15 15 __ __ __   20 20 __ __ __

CIRCLE THE SAME WORD.

1. address	dress	(address)	abyss
2. street	streak	treats	street
3. number	number	member	numeral
4. road	read	road	need
5. city	cite	city	yet
6. state	start	staff	state

WRITE YOUR ADDRESS.

1. ADDRESS _____
           NUMBER   STREET

2. _____
Address: Number   Street

3.
number   street

4. Address _____
        Number   Street

_____
City   State   Zip Code

SPEAKING PRACTICE

1.

2.

3.

4.

WRITE YOUR TELEPHONE NUMBER.

1. Telephone number _____

2. Telephone: _____

3. _____
   Phone number

📼 LISTEN AND CIRCLE THE NUMBERS YOU HEAR.

1. (7)   11

2. 10   12

3. 19   9

4. 13   14

5. 6   9

6.   753–8463   573–4863

7.   762–8137   752–3781

8.   533–3577   353–8511

9.   686–5307   686–0945

10.   425–9713   524–3718

FILL OUT THE FORM.

Name _____
   First   Last

Address _____
   Number   Street

   _____
   City   State   Zip Code

Telephone _____

1. supermarket   **2.** bank   **3.** clinic

DRAW A LINE.

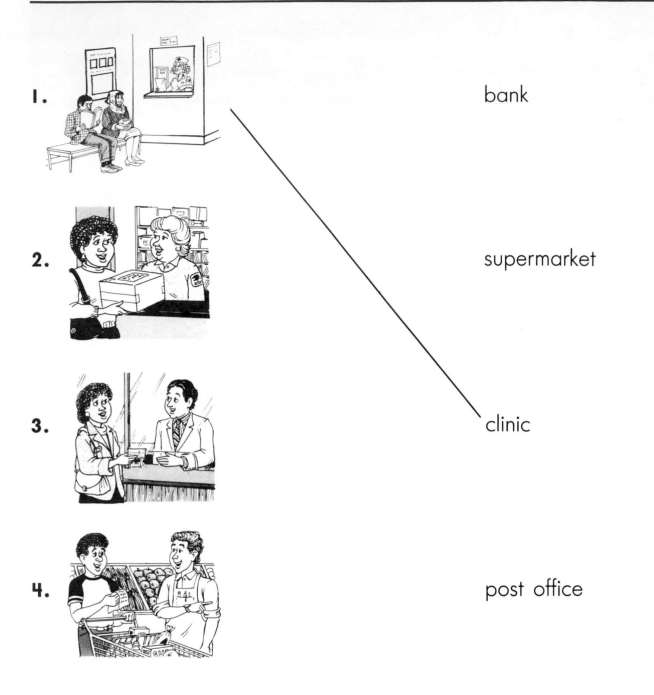

1.   bank

2.   supermarket

3.   clinic

4.   post office

📼 LISTEN AND CIRCLE THE STREET YOU HEAR.

1. (Main Street)   (River Road)   4. (Central Avenue) (First Avenue)

2. (K Street)   (B Street)   5. (K Street)   (Main Street)

3. (Park Road)   (River Road)   6. (West Avenue)   (Wilson Avenue)

72

SPEAKING PRACTICE

the post office

the laundromat

the clinic   the bank

1.

school   the supermarket

2.

the bus stop   the park

3.

the post office   the movies

4.

WRITE THE CORRECT WORD UNDER THE PICTURE.

bank	bus stop	clinic	laundromat
movies	park	post office	school

1. _____park_____

2. _____

3. _____

4. _____

5. _____

6. _____

7. _____

8. _____

74

☰ LISTEN AND PUT AN X UNDER THE CORRECT PICTURE.

1. _____ X _____   **2.** _____ _____

3. _____ _____   **4.** _____ _____

5. _____ _____   **6.** _____ _____

NUMBER REVIEW: FILL IN THE MISSING NUMBERS.

1   2   3   ___   5   6   ___

8   9   ___   11   ___   ___   14

___   16   17   ___   ___   20

WRITE THE NUMBERS FROM 1 TO 20.

1 ___ ___ ___ ___ ___ ___ ___ ___ ___

___ ___ ___ ___ ___ ___ ___ ___ ___ ___

COUNT TO 100. FILL IN THE MISSING NUMBERS.

	1	2	3	4	5	6	7	8	9
10	11	12	13	14	15	16	17	18	19
20	21	22	23	24	25	26	27	28	29
30	31	_32_	33	34	___	36	___	38	39
40	41	42	___	44	45	___	47	___	___
50	___	52	53	___	___	56	___	58	___
60	___	___	63	64	___	66	___	___	___
70	71	___	___	___	75	___	___	___	___
80	___	___	___	___	___	___	___	___	___
90	___	___	___	___	___	___	___	___	___
100

SPEAKING PRACTICE

1.

2.

3.

4.

LOOK AT THE PICTURES.   DRAW A LINE.

Buses: 30 WESTVILLE   27 WASHINGTON   72 EASTON   42 RYE   64 RIVERSIDE

1.	Riverside	30
2.	Westville	27
3.	Easton	42
4.	Rye	64
5.	Washington	72

🔲 LISTEN AND CIRCLE THE NUMBER YOU HEAR.

1. (29)   36   **5.**   42   24

2. 13   32   **6.**   45   59

3. 16   53   **7.**   65   25

4. 7   11   **8.**   15   50

WRITE THE NAME OF THE STREET.

1. My home is on _____.

2. My school is on _____.

3. The post office is on _____.

4. The supermarket is on _____.

78

A. Excuse me. What time is it?
B. 2:00.
A. Did you say 2:00?
B. Yes. That's right.
A. Thank you.

1.

2.

3.

4.

5.

6.

CIRCLE THE SAME TIME.

1.	(2:00)	2:30	3:00	7:00
2.	3:00	4:00	8:00	6:00
3.	12:00	7:00	4:00	10:00
4.	6:00	8:30	4:00	4:30
5.	7:00	10:00	1:00	11:00
6.	9:30	6:00	3:30	10:30
7.	1:30	11:00	12:30	11:30
8.	12:30	6:00	1:30	12:00

READ AND COPY.

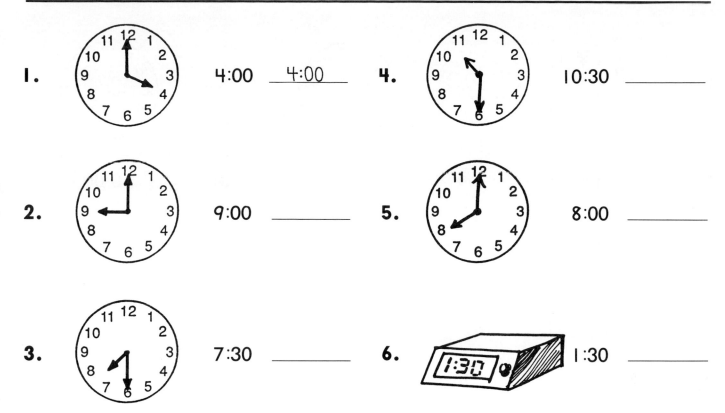

1. 4:00 _4:00_

2. 9:00 _____

3. 7:30 _____

4. 10:30 _____

5. 8:00 _____

6. 1:30 _____

WRITE THE TIME.

1. _4:00_   2. _____   3. _____   4. _____

5. _____   6. _____   7. _____   8. _____

DRAW THE TIME ON THE CLOCK.

1.   1:00

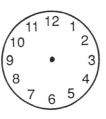

2.   8:00

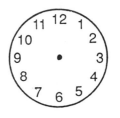

3.   10:00

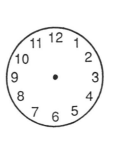

4.   3:30

5.   5:00

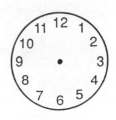

6.   11:30

 LISTEN AND CHECK THE TIME YOU HEAR.

1. _____   ✔

2. _____   _____

3. _____   _____

4. _____   _____

5. _____   _____

6. _____   _____

82

SPEAKING PRACTICE

A. Can you come in on Friday at 2:00?
B. Friday at 2:00? Yes. That's fine.
A. Good. See you then.

1. Monday at 9:00?

2. Wednesday at 1:30?

3. Saturday at 10:30?

4. Thursday at 4:00?

READ AND COPY.

1. Sunday   Sunday   _____

2. Monday   Monday   _____

3. Tuesday   Tuesday   _____

4. Wednesday   Wednesday   _____

5. Thursday   Thursday   _____

6. Friday   Friday   _____

7. Saturday   Saturday   _____

DRAW A LINE.

1.	Sunday	Mon.
2.	Thursday	Wed.
3.	Wednesday	Sat.
4.	Saturday	Fri.
5.	Tuesday	Sun.
6.	Monday	Thurs.
7.	Friday	Tues.

LOOK AT THE CALENDAR. FILL IN THE DAYS.

Sunday	Monday	Tuesday	Wednesday	Thursday	Friday	Saturday
		1	2	3	4	5
6	7	8	9	10	11	12
13	14	15	16	17	18	19
20	21	22	23	24	25	26
27	28	29	30	31		

1. Sunday   _Monday_   Tuesday   Wednesday

_____   Friday   _____

2. _____   Monday   _____   _____

Thursday   _____   Saturday

🖭 LISTEN AND CHECK.

1. _✔_ Monday
___ Sunday

4. ___ Wed.
___ Mon.

2. ___ Tuesday
___ Thursday

5. ___ Fri.
___ Sat.

3. ___ Saturday
___ Sunday

6. ___ Thurs.
___ Tues.

MARIA'S CALENDAR

Sun.	Mon.	Tues.	Wed.	Thurs.	Fri.	Sat.
1	2	3	4	5	6	7
8	9 school 12:30	10	11 school 12:30	12 clinic 9:00	13 bank	14 movies 7:30

WHERE ARE YOU GOING NEXT WEEK? WHAT TIME? WRITE IT ON THE CALENDAR.

bank	clinic	movies
post office	school	supermarket

Sunday	Monday	Tuesday	Wednesday	Thursday	Friday	Saturday

A. What's the matter?

B. My arm hurts.

A. Okay. Please take a seat. The doctor will see you soon.

1. leg

2. head

3. back

4. stomach

5. foot

6. ear

87

LOOK AT THE PICTURE AND READ.

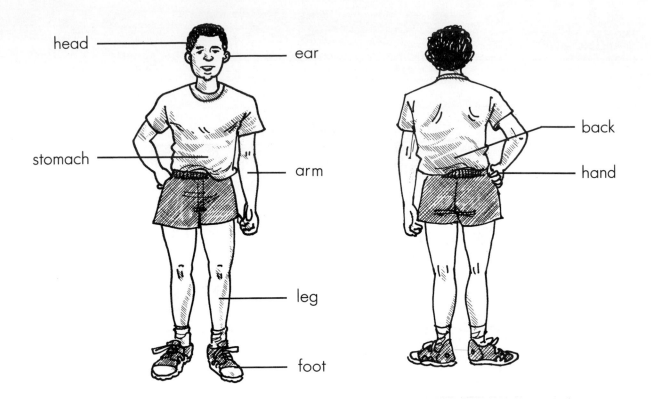

head — ear

stomach — arm

back

hand

leg

foot

DRAW A LINE.

1. foot

2. hand

3. leg

4. head

5. stomach

6. arm

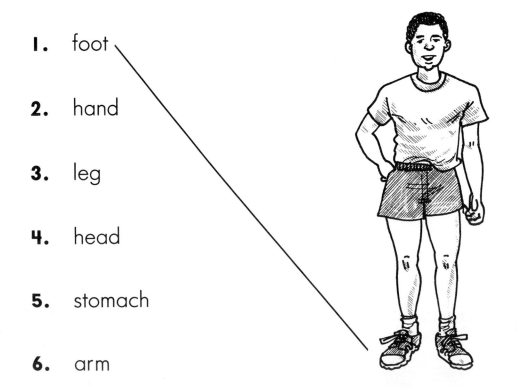

SPEAKING PRACTICE

A. Here's your medicine. Take 1 tablet 3 times a day.
B. I understand. 1 tablet 3 times a day. Thank you.

1. Take 2 tablets 4 times a day.

2. Take 1 teaspoon every 6 hours.

3. Take 2 capsules every day.

4. Take 1 pill 3 times a day.

DRAW A LINE.

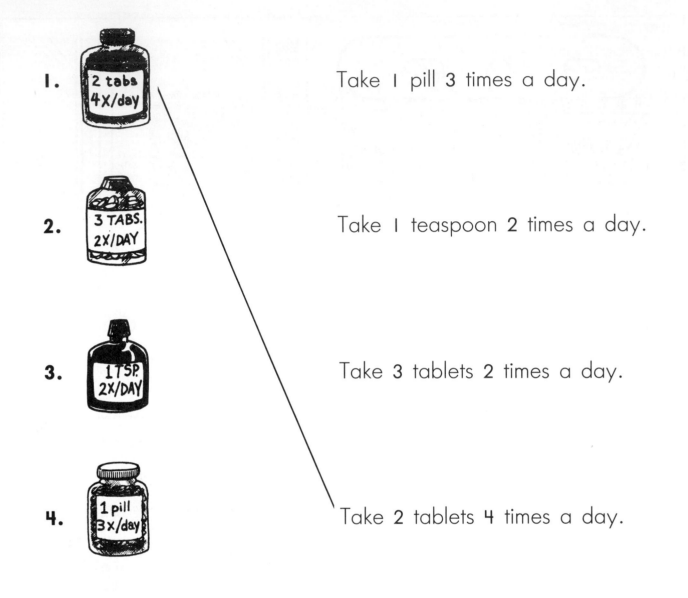

1. [2 tabs 4X/day]   Take 1 pill 3 times a day.

2. [3 TABS. 2X/DAY]   Take 1 teaspoon 2 times a day.

3. [1 TSP. 2X/DAY]   Take 3 tablets 2 times a day.

4. [1 pill 3X/day]   Take 2 tablets 4 times a day.

LISTEN AND WRITE THE NUMBER YOU HEAR.

1. Take ___2___ tablets.

2. Take _____ teaspoons.

3. Take _____ capsules.

4. Take _____ teaspoon.

5. Take 1 capsule every _____ hours.

6. Take 1 tablet _____ times a day.

7. Take 2 teaspoons _____ times a day.

8. Take _____ capsules every _____ hours.

SPEAKING PRACTICE

A. Emergency Operator.

B. My father is having a heart attack!

A. What's your name?

B. Diane Perkins.

A. Address?

B. 76 Lake Street.

A. Phone number?

B. 293-7637.

A. We'll be right there.

1. Carmen Diaz
1440 Lexington Street
354-6260

2. Janet Brown
17 Park Road
963-2475

3. Henry Stewart
5 Linden Road
723-0980

4. Nancy Stockman
193 Davis Avenue
458-9313

INTERVIEW 3 PEOPLE.

What's your name?
What's your address?
What's your phone number?

1. Name _____

   Address _____

   _____

   Phone number _____

2. NAME _____
      Last   First

   ADDRESS _____

   _____

   PHONE _____

3. Name

   Address

   Phone

92

A. That'll be $2.00.

B. $2.00?

A. Yes. That's right.

B. Here you are.

A. Thank you. Have a nice day.

1. $4.00

2. $1.00

3.   25¢

4. $3.10

5.   80¢

6. $10.15

READ AND COPY.

1. a penny

1¢   1¢   1¢ _____

$ .01 $ .01   _____

2. a nickel

5¢   5¢   _____

$ .05 $ .05   _____

3. a dime

10¢   10¢   _____

$ .10 $ .10   _____

4. a quarter

25¢   25¢   _____

$ .25 $ .25   _____

5. a half-dollar

50¢   50¢   _____

$ .50 $ .50   _____

6. a dollar bill

$1.00 $1.00   _____

COUNT THE MONEY.

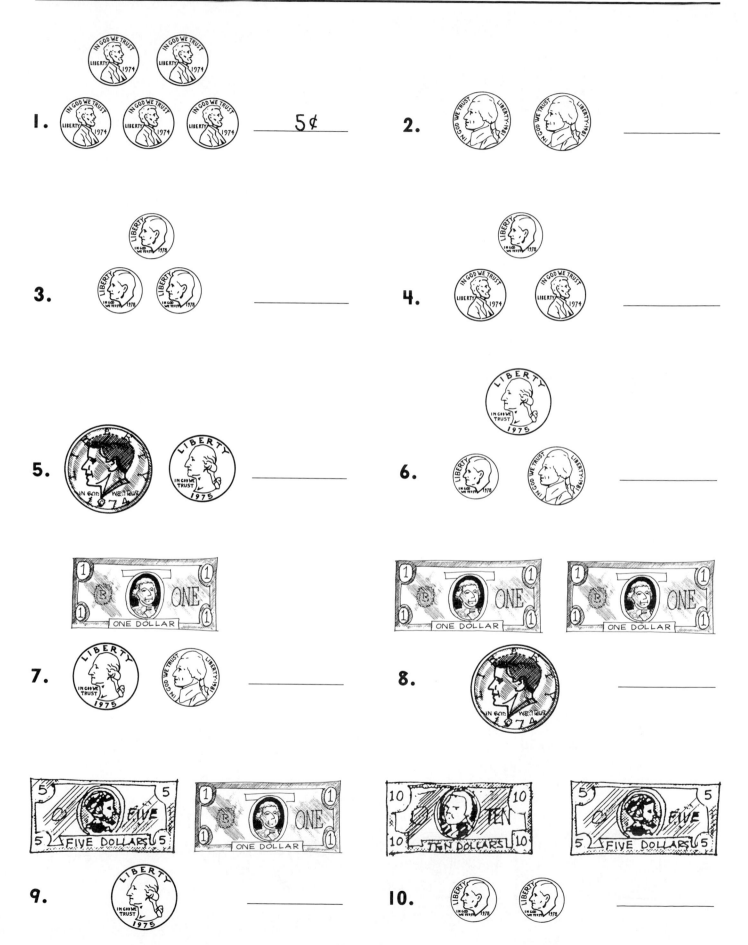

1.   5¢ _____

2. _____

3. _____

4. _____

5. _____

6. _____

7. _____

8. _____

9. _____

10. _____

DRAW A LINE.

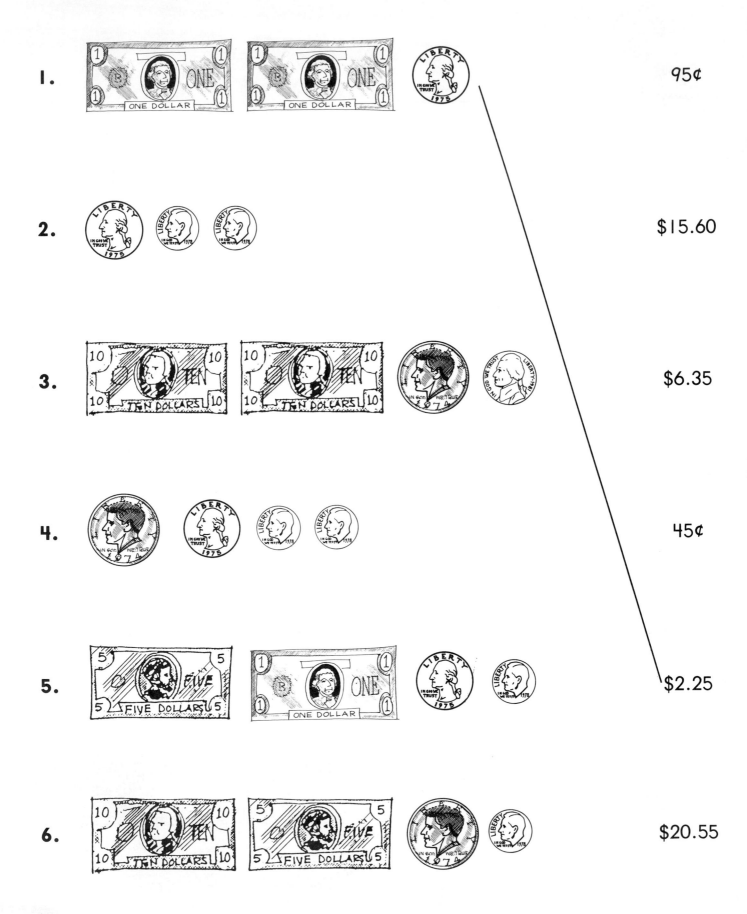

1. 95¢

2. $15.60

3. $6.35

4. 45¢

5. $2.25

6. $20.55

1. $3.15   ($30.65)   **4.** $8.40 $3.84

2. $10.20 $2.22   **5.** $6.55 $9.89

3. $44.75 $24.25   **6.** $19.00 $1.19

![cassette] **LISTEN AND DRAW AN X UNDER THE CORRECT PICTURE.**

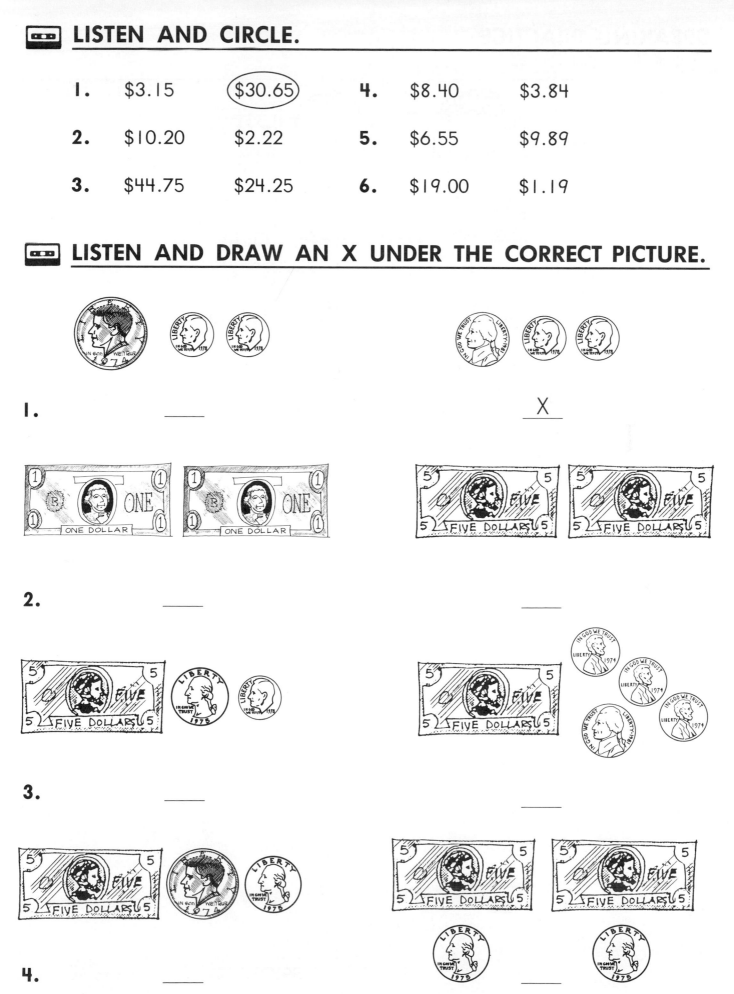

1.   _____   X

2.   _____   _____

3.   _____   _____

4.   _____   _____

SPEAKING PRACTICE

A. May I help you?

B. Yes, please. How much is this shirt?

A. It's $7.99.

B. Thank you.

1. dress
$22.45

2. hat
$13.56

3. jacket
$35.75

4. umbrella
$9.29

▣ LISTEN AND WRITE THE AMOUNT YOU HEAR.

1. <u>$6.59</u>

2. _____

3. _____

4. _____

5. _____

6. _____

7. _____

8. _____

▣ LISTEN AND CHOOSE THE CORRECT PICTURE.

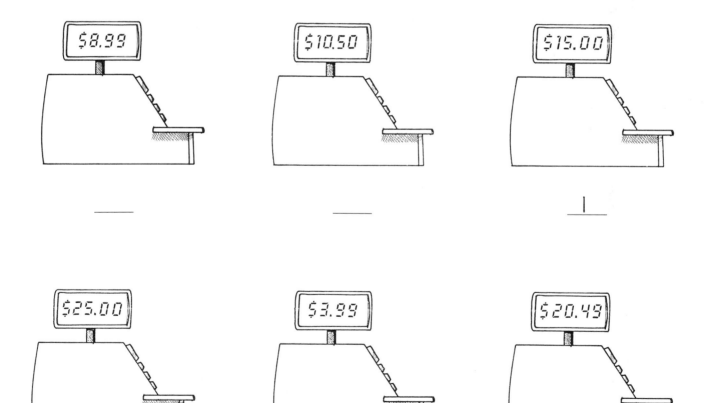

LOOK AT THE PICTURES AND ANSWER THE QUESTIONS.

 $8.59

$17.00

 $6.95

 $39.99

 $5.89

1. How much is this hat? _____ $6.95 _____

2. How much is this jacket? _____

3. How much is this shirt? _____

4. How much is this umbrella? _____

5. How much is this dress? _____

JOBS

A. I saw your sign. What job do you have open?

B. We're looking for a cook.

A. I'd like to apply.

B. Do you have experience?

A. Yes, I do.

B. Okay. Here's an application form.

1. cashier

2. mechanic

3. waiter

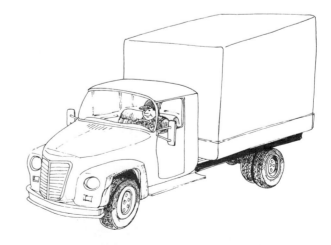

4. driver

DRAW A LINE.

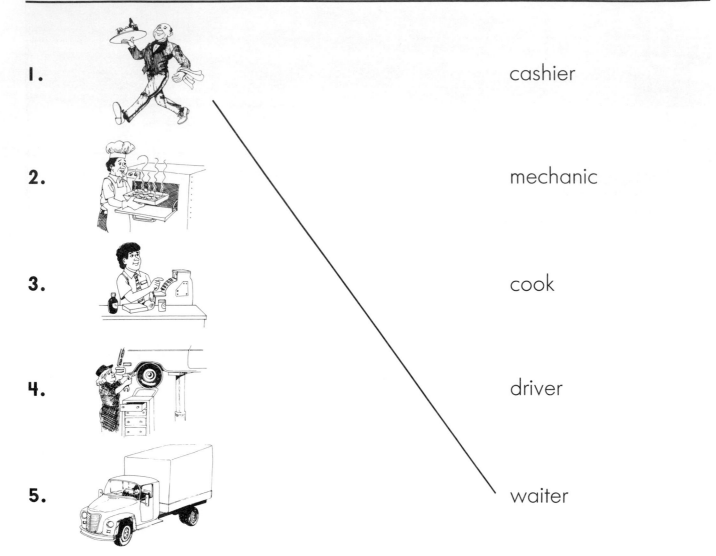

1.

2.

3.

4.

5.

cashier

mechanic

cook

driver

waiter

🔲 LISTEN AND WRITE THE NUMBER UNDER THE PICTURE.

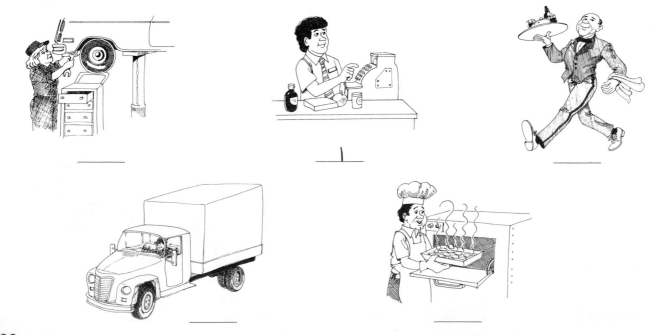

FILL IN THE APPLICATION FORMS.

I.

Acme Company
Employment Application Form

Name: _____
 last   first

Address: _____
 number   street

 _____
 city   state   zip code

Telephone: _____

Age: _____

Do you have experience?   Yes _____   No _____

2.

DALTON COMPANY
Employment Application Form

Name
Last   First

Address
Number   Street

City   State   Zip Code

Telephone [ ][ ][ ] - [ ][ ][ ][ ]   Age [ ][ ]

Do you have experience?   Yes [ ]   No [ ]

SPEAKING PRACTICE

A. What are the hours?

B. 9:00 to 5:30.

A. And how much is the salary?

B. $5.00 an hour.

A. I see. I'd like to apply.

1.   8:30 - 5:00 $6.00 an hour

2.   7:30 - 6:00 $50.00 a day

3.   8:00 - 12:00 $8.25 an hour

4.   7:00 - 3:30 $280 a week

READ THE JOB ANNOUNCEMENTS. DRAW A LINE.

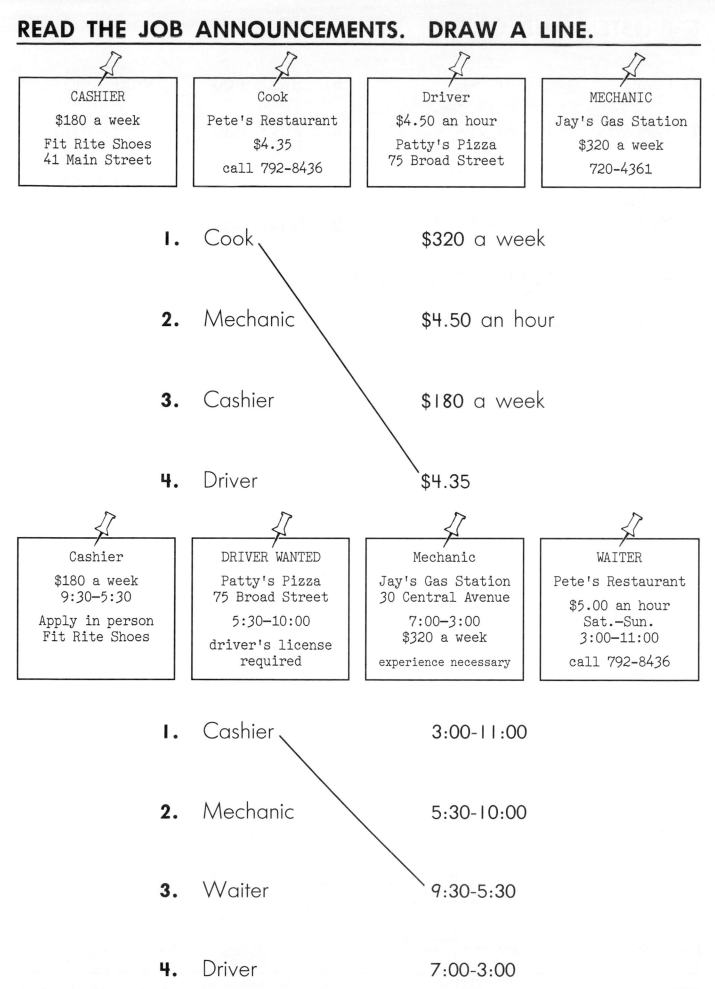

CASHIER	Cook	Driver	MECHANIC
$180 a week	Pete's Restaurant	$4.50 an hour	Jay's Gas Station
Fit Rite Shoes 41 Main Street	$4.35 call 792-8436	Patty's Pizza 75 Broad Street	$320 a week 720-4361

1. Cook $320 a week

2. Mechanic $4.50 an hour

3. Cashier $180 a week

4. Driver $4.35

Cashier	DRIVER WANTED	Mechanic	WAITER
$180 a week 9:30–5:30	Patty's Pizza 75 Broad Street	Jay's Gas Station 30 Central Avenue	Pete's Restaurant
Apply in person Fit Rite Shoes	5:30–10:00 driver's license required	7:00–3:00 $320 a week experience necessary	$5.00 an hour Sat.–Sun. 3:00–11:00 call 792-8436

1. Cashier   3:00–11:00

2. Mechanic   5:30–10:00

3. Waiter   9:30–5:30

4. Driver   7:00–3:00

🔊 LISTEN AND CIRCLE.

1. (($3.80)) $8.50   5. 9:30–5:00   9:00–5:30

2. $4.25 $5.75   6. 7:30–3:30   11:30–6:30

3. $630 $360   7. 10:00–2:00   7:00–12:00

4. $255 $10.25   8. 9:00–5:00   6:00–9:00

FILL IN THE APPLICATION FORM.

EMPLOYMENT APPLICATION

Social Security Number _____

NAME _____
        FIRST NAME   MIDDLE INITIAL   LAST NAME

STREET ADDRESS _____

CITY _____ STATE _____ ZIP _____

TELEPHONE: _____ _____
            AREA CODE   NUMBER

AVAILABILITY

		M	T	W	T	F	S	S
HOURS AVAILABLE	FROM							
	TO							

MOST RECENT JOB

NAME OF COMPANY _____

JOB _____ NAME OF SUPERVISOR _____

SALARY _____

SIGNS

8

A. Excuse me. Can I park here?
B. No. There's the sign.
A. Oh, okay. Thank you.

1. smoke

2. fish

3. swim

4. eat

READ THE SIGNS. DRAW A LINE.

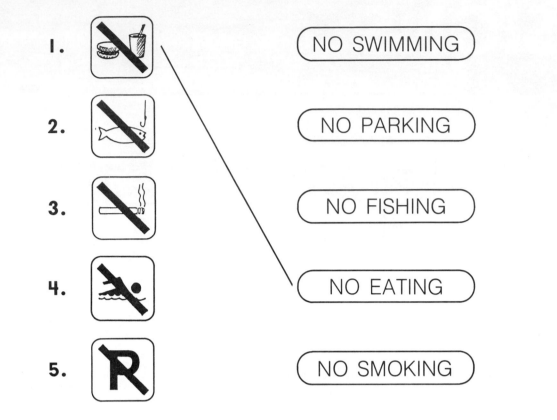

1.   NO SWIMMING

2.   NO PARKING

3.   NO FISHING

4.   NO EATING

5.   NO SMOKING

🔊 LISTEN AND DRAW AN X UNDER THE CORRECT PICTURE.

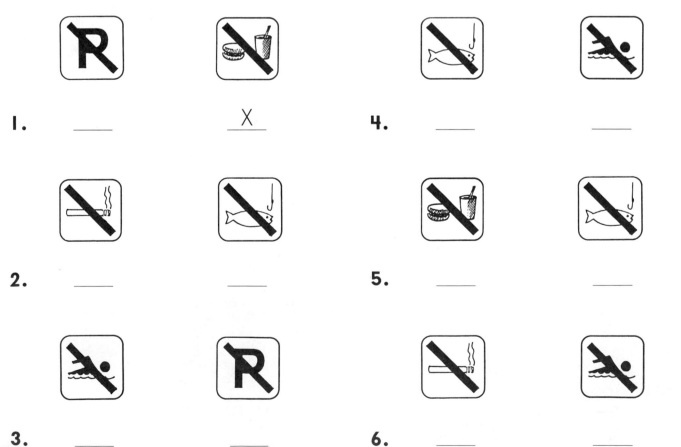

🎦 LISTEN AND CIRCLE.

1. (NO PARKING) ((NO FISHING))
2. (NO EATING) (NO SMOKING)
3. (NO FISHING) (NO SWIMMING)

4. (NO SMOKING) (NO PARKING)
5. (NO SWIMMING) (NO SMOKING)
6. (NO FISHING) (NO EATING)

WRITE THE CORRECT WORDS UNDER THE PICTURE.

1.

NO FISHING

2.

_____

3.

_____

4.

_____

5.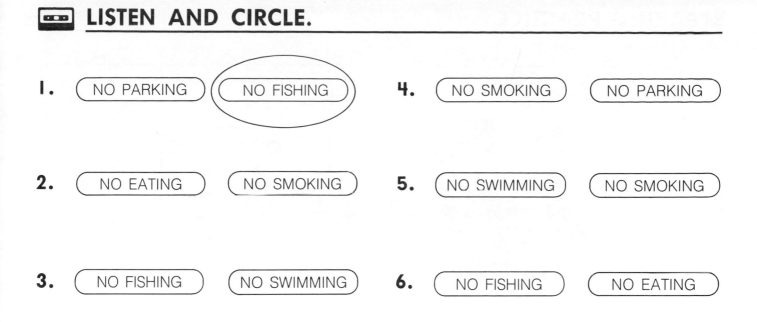

_____

SPEAKING PRACTICE

men's room?

A. Excuse me. Where's the men's room?
B. It's over there. Do you see the sign?
A. Oh, yes. I see it. Thank you.

1. ladies' room?

2. telephone?

3. parking lot?

4. lunch room?

DRAW A LINE.

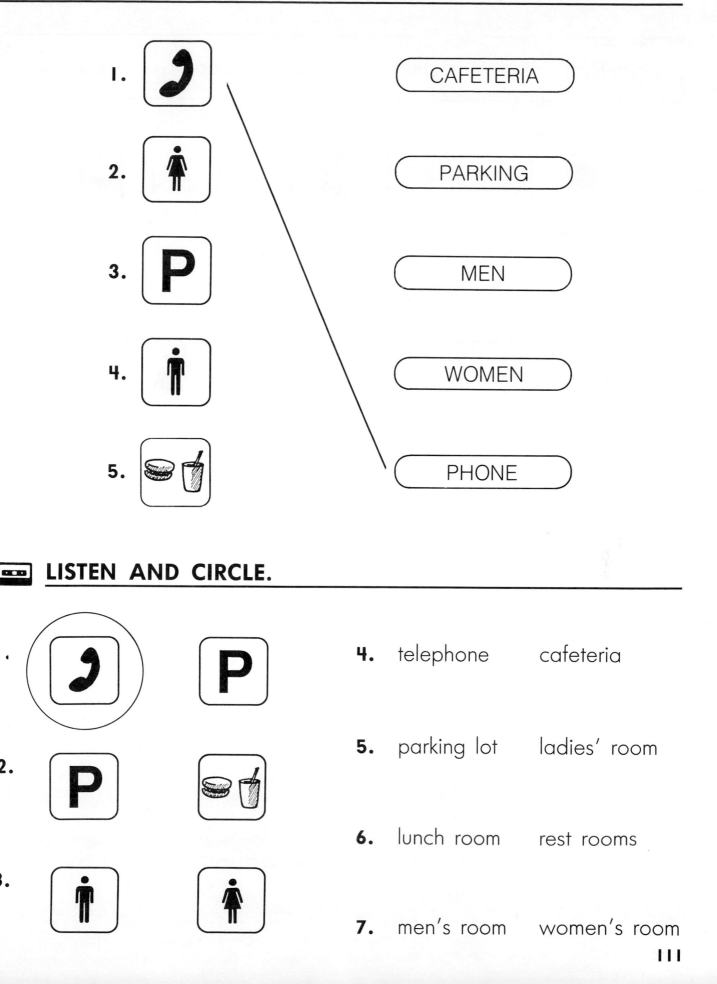

1. (phone icon)

2. (women icon)

3. P

4. (man icon)

5. (food tray icon)

CAFETERIA

PARKING

MEN

WOMEN

PHONE

🔲 LISTEN AND CIRCLE.

1. (phone icon - circled)   P

2. P   (food tray icon)

3. (man icon)   (woman icon)

4. telephone   cafeteria

5. parking lot   ladies' room

6. lunch room   rest rooms

7. men's room   women's room

WRITE THE CORRECT WORDS UNDER THE PICTURE.

| cafeteria | ladies' room | men's room | parking | telephone |

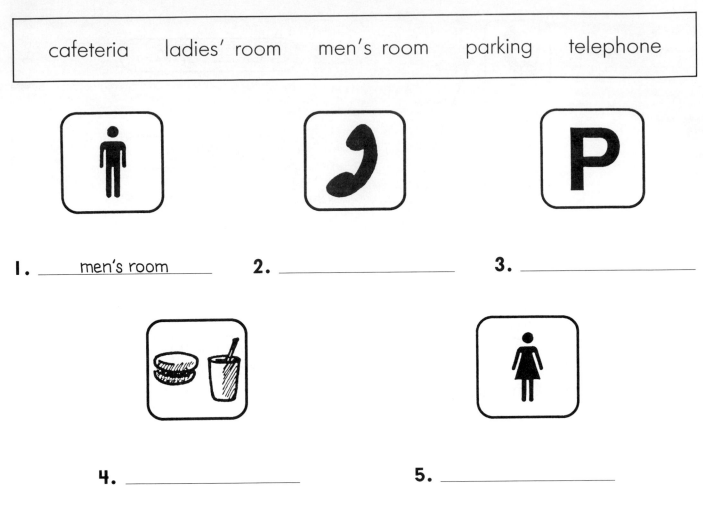

1. ___men's room___

2. _____

3. _____

4. _____

5. _____

DRAW 3 SIGNS YOU SEE EVERY DAY.

FRIENDS

9

A. Do you want to do something on Friday?

B. On Friday? I can't. I have to go to the clinic.

A. How about Monday?

B. Monday? Okay.

1.

2.

3.

4.

WRITE THE CORRECT WORD UNDER THE PICTURE.

| airport | clinic | hospital | laundromat | supermarket |

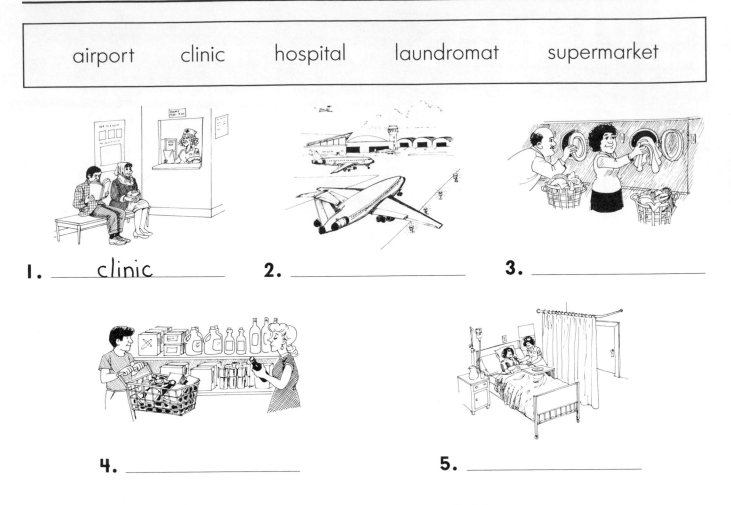

1. clinic

2. _____

3. _____

4. _____

5. _____

REVIEW: WRITE THE DAYS OF THE WEEK.

Sun.	Mon.	Tues.	Wed.	Thurs.	Fri.	Sat.
4	5	6	7	8	9	10

1. Sun. = _____Sunday_____

2. Mon.= _____

3. Tues.= _____

4. Wed.= _____

5. Thurs.= _____

6. Fri. = _____

7. Sat. = _____

114

1. clinic (airport)   5. Monday   Sunday

2. laundromat   supermarket   6. Saturday   Thursday

3. hospital   clinic   7. Fri.   Wed.

4. supermarket   airport   8. Tues.   Thurs.

■■ **LISTEN AND WRITE ON THE CALENDAR.**

| airport | clinic | hospital | laundromat | supermarket |

Sun.	Mon.	Tues.	Wed.	Thurs.	Fri.	Sat.
4	5	6	7	8	9	10
	laundromat					

REVIEW: WRITE THE TIME.

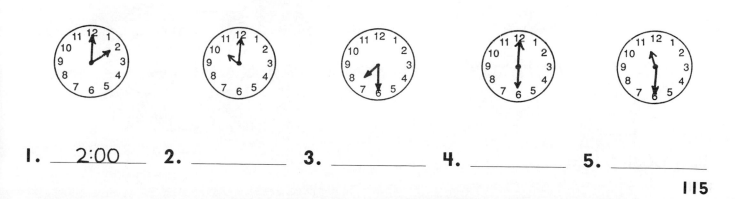

1. __2:00__   2. _____   3. _____   4. _____   5. _____

SPEAKING PRACTICE

airport

A. What time is it?

B. It's 1:30.

A. Oh! I have to get to the airport!

B. See you soon.

A. Good-bye.

1. laundromat

2. bank

3. post office

4. clinic

CIRCLE THE SAME TIME.

1.	4:30	(2:30)	4:00	6:15
2.	2:00	11:00	7:15	3:00
3.	11:45	7:15	8:00	8:30
4.	12:00	12:30	1:30	6:00
5.	9:15	9:30	5:45	4:45
6.	4:00	12:30	12:00	8:00
7.	3:30	6:15	8:15	3:00
8.	2:45	2:00	9:15	3:45
9.	12:00	12:15	3:30	3:00
10.	5:45	10:30	9:30	6:45

Bank Hours **9:00–2:00** **Mon.-Fri.**	**Bank Hours** **8:30–3:30** **Mon.-Fri.**

1. _____ ___X___

CLINIC Business Hours 7:15–5:45	CLINIC Business Hours 7:45–5:15

2. _____ _____

Post Office **open** **8:30–5:00**	**POST OFFICE** **hours** **8:15–4:45**

3. _____ _____

Eat-Rite Supermarket Mon.-Sat. 8:00–8:00 Sun. 1:00–5:00	Save-Way Supermarket Mon.-Fri. 8:00–6:00 Sat. 8:00–7:00 Sun. closed

4. _____ _____

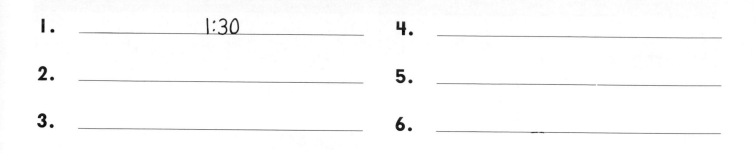

📼 LISTEN AND WRITE THE TIME.

1. _____ 1:30 _____   4. _____

2. _____   5. _____

3. _____   6. _____

WRITE YOUR ENGLISH CLASS SCHEDULE.

Class Schedule

DAY	TIME	
	From	To
Monday		
Tuesday		
Wednesday		
Thursday		
Friday		
Saturday		
Sunday		

Write the hours of your supermarket.

	From	To
Mon.	____	____
Tues.	____	____
Wed.	____	____
Thurs.	____	____
Fri.	____	____
Sat.	____	____
Sun.	____	____

Write the hours of your post office.

	From	To
Mon.	____	____
Tues.	____	____
Wed.	____	____
Thurs.	____	____
Fri.	____	____
Sat.	____	____
Sun.	____	____

DIALOGS: CHAPTERS 1, 2, & 3

CHAPTER 1

Page 35

A. Hello. My name is Carlos Martinez.

B. Hi. I'm Kim Park. Nice to meet you.

A. Nice to meet you, too.

Page 38

A. What's your last name?

B. Sanchez.

A. How do you spell it?

B. S-A-N-C-H-E-Z.

Page 56

A. This is my husband, Michael.

B. Hello, Michael. Nice to meet you.

CHAPTER 2

Page 59

A. What's your son's name?

B. David.

A. How old is he?

B. He's 6.

A. What's your daughter's name?

B. Maria.

A. How old is she?

B. She's 10.

Page 66

A. What's your address?

B. 14 Main Street.

Page 69

A. What's your telephone number?

B. 432-6978.

CHAPTER 3

Page 71

A. Where's the post office?

B. It's on Main Street.

Page 73

A. Hi. How are you?

B. Fine. And you?

A. Fine, thanks. Where are you going?

B. To the laundromat. How about you?

A. I'm going to the post office.

Page 77

A. Do you go to Main Street?

B. No. Take Bus Number 25.

SCRIPTS FOR LISTENING EXERCISES

Page 54

Listen and circle the letters you hear.

1. A-S
2. M-E
3. F-I-R
4. T-O-M
5. J-O-A-N
6. l-a-s-t
7. n-a-m-e
8. f-i-r-s-t
9. Capital K-a-r-e-n
10. Capital B-l-a-n-c-o

Page 54

Listen and write the names you hear.

1. Kim. Capital K-i-m.
2. Sue. Capital S-u-e.
3. Tom. Capital T-o-m.
4. Jane. Capital J-a-n-e.
5. Linda. Capital L-i-n-d-a.
6. Nancy. Capital N-a-n-c-y.
7. Smith. Capital S-m-i-t-h.
8. Robert. Capital R-o-b-e-r-t.
9. Wilson. Capital W-i-l-s-o-n.
10. Johnson. Capital J-o-h-n-s-o-n.

Page 58

Listen and write an X under the correct picture.

1. A. This is my mother, Mrs. Brown.
   B. Nice to meet you, Mrs. Brown.
2. A. This is my wife, Mary.
   B. Nice to meet you, Mary.
3. A. This is my husband, John.
   B. Nice to meet you, John.
4. A. This is my daughter, Susan.
   B. Nice to meet you, Susan.
5. A. This is my son, Charles.
   B. Nice to meet you, Charles.
6. A. This is my father, Mr. Smith.
   B. Nice to meet you, Mr. Smith.

Page 70

Listen and circle the numbers you hear.

1. A. What's your address?
   B. Seven Main Street.
2. A. What's your address?
   B. Twelve First Avenue.
3. A. What's your address?
   B. Nine Center Street.
4. A. What's your address?
   B. Thirteen B Street.
5. A. What's your address?
   B. Six Park Avenue.
6. A. What's your telephone number?
   B. Five seven three - four eight six three.
7. A. What's your telephone number?
   B. Seven six two - eight one three seven.
8. A. What's your telephone number?
   B. Three five three - eight five one one.
9. A. What's your number?
   B. Six eight six - five three "oh" seven.
10. A. Phone number?
    B. Four two five - nine seven one three.

Page 72

Listen and circle the street you hear.

1. A. Where's the post office?
   B. It's on Main Street.
2. A. Where's the bank?
   B. It's on B Street.
3. A. Where's the clinic?
   B. It's on River Road.
4. A. Where's the supermarket?
   B. It's on First Avenue.
5. A. Where's the office?
   B. It's on Main Street.
6. A. Where's the market?
   B. It's on Wilson Avenue.

Page 75

Listen and put an X under the correct picture.

1. A. Where are you going?
   B. To the movies.
2. A. Where are you going?
   B. To the supermarket.
3. A. Where are you going?
   B. To school.
4. A. Where are you going?
   B. I'm going to the bank.
5. A. Where are you going?
   B. I'm going to the park.
6. A. Where are you going?
   B. To the clinic.

Page 78

Listen and circle the number you hear.

1. A. Do you go to Main Street?
   B. No. Take Bus Number twenty-nine.
2. A. Do you go to Westville?
   B. No. Take Bus Number thirty-two.
3. A. Do you go to the park?
   B. No. Take Bus Number fifty-three.
4. A. Do you go to Riverside?
   B. No. Take Bus Number seven.
5. A. Do you go to First Street?
   B. No. Take Bus Number forty-two.
6. A. Do you go to F Street?
   B. No. Take Bus Number fifty-nine.
7. A. Do you go to Ocean Street?
   B. No. Take Bus Number sixty-five.
8. A. Do you go to Wilson Road?
   B. No. Take Bus Number fifteen.

Page 82

Listen and check the time you hear.

1. A. What time is it?
   B. Ten o'clock.
   A. Did you say ten o'clock?
   B. Yes. That's right.
2. A. What time is it?
   B. Two thirty.
   A. Did you say two thirty?
   B. Yes. That's right.
3. A. What time is it?
   B. Eleven o'clock.
   A. Did you say eleven o'clock?
   B. Yes. That's right.
4. A. What time is it?
   B. Two o'clock.
5. A. What time is it?
   B. Five thirty.
6. A. Did you say six o'clock?
   B. Yes. That's right.

Page 85

Listen and check.

1. A. Can you come in on Monday?
   B. Monday? Yes. That's fine.
2. A. Can you come in on Tuesday?
   B. Tuesday? Yes. That's fine.
3. A. Can you come in on Sunday?
   B. Sunday? Yes. That's fine.
4. Can you come in on Wednesday at two o'clock?
5. Can you come in on Saturday at nine thirty?
6. Can you come in on Thursday at ten o'clock?

Page 90

Listen and write the number you hear.

1. A. Here's your medicine. Take two tablets every day.
   B. Two tablets every day. Thank you.
2. A. Here's your medicine. Take two teaspoons two times a day.
   B. Two teaspoons two times a day. Thank you.
3. A. Take three capsules two times a day.
   B. Three capsules two times a day. Thank you.

4. A. Take one teaspoon three times a day.
   B. One teaspoon three times a day.

5. A. Take one capsule every three hours.
   B. One capsule every three hours.

6. A. Take one tablet two times a day.
   B. One tablet two times a day.

7. A. Take two teaspoons four times a day.
   B. Two teaspoons four times a day.

8. A. Take two capsules every three hours.
   B. Two capsules every three hours.

Page 97

Listen and circle.

1. A. That'll be thirty dollars and sixty-five cents.
   B. Thirty dollars and sixty-five cents?
   A. Yes. That's right.

2. A. That'll be ten dollars and twenty cents.
   B. Ten dollars and twenty cents?
   A. Yes. That's right.

3. A. That'll be forty-four dollars and seventy-five cents.
   B. Forty-four dollars and seventy-five cents?
   A. Yes. That's right.

4. A. That'll be three dollars and eighty-four cents.
   B. Three dollars and eighty-four cents?
   A. Yes. That's right.

5. That'll be six dollars and fifty-five cents.

6. That'll be one dollar and nineteen cents.

Page 97

Listen and draw an X under the correct picture.

1. A. That'll be twenty-five cents.
   B. Twenty-five cents?
   A. Yes. That's right.

2. A. That'll be two dollars.
   B. Two dollars?
   A. Yes. That's right.

3. A. That'll be five dollars and thirty-five cents.
   B. Five dollars and thirty-five cents?
   A. Yes. That's right.

4. A. That'll be ten dollars and fifty cents.
   B. Ten dollars and fifty cents?
   A. Yes. That's right.

Page 99

Listen and write the amount you hear.

1. A. How much is this shirt?
   B. It's six dollars and fifty-nine cents.
   A. Six dollars and fifty-nine cents? Thank you.

2. A. How much is this umbrella?
   B. It's five dollars.
   A. Five dollars? Thank you.

3. A. How much is this hat?
   B. It's two dollars.
   A. Two dollars? Thank you.

4. A. That'll be four dollars and fifty cents.
   B. Four dollars and fifty cents?
   A. Yes. That's right.

5. A. That'll be three dollars and seventy-five cents.
   B. Three dollars and seventy-five cents?
   A. Yes. That's right.

6. A. How much is this jacket?
   B. It's twelve dollars and ninety-five cents.
   A. Twelve dollars and ninety-five cents? Thank you.

7. A. How much is this dress?
   B. It's thirty-five dollars and twenty-nine cents.
   A. Thirty-five dollars and twenty-nine cents? Thank you.

8. A. That'll be fifty-six dollars and eighty-four cents.
   B. Fifty-six dollars and eighty-four cents?
   A. Yes. That's right.

Page 99

Listen and choose the correct picture.

1. A. How much is this jacket?
   B. It's fifteen dollars.

2. A. How much is this dress?
   B. It's twenty-five dollars.

3. That'll be ten dollars and fifty cents.

4. That'll be three dollars and ninety-nine cents.

5. A. How much is this umbrella?
   B. It's eight dollars and ninety-nine cents.

6. That'll be twenty dollars and forty-nine cents.

Page 102

Listen and write the number under the picture.

1. A. I saw your sign. What job do you have open?
   B. We're looking for a cashier.

2. A. I saw your sign. What job do you have open?
   B. We're looking for a cook.

3. A. I saw your sign. What job do you have open?
   B. We're looking for a waiter.

4. A. What job do you have open?
   B. We're looking for a mechanic.

5. A. What job do you have open?
   B. We're looking for a driver.

Page 106

Listen and circle.

1. A. How much is the salary?
   B. Three dollars and eighty cents an hour.

A. Three dollars and eighty cents?
B. Yes. That's right.

2. A. How much is the salary?
   B. Five dollars and seventy-five cents.

A. Five dollars and seventy-five cents?
B. Yes. That's right.

3. A. How much is the salary?
   B. Three hundred sixty dollars a week.

A. Three hundred sixty dollars?
B. Yes. That's right.

4. A. How much is the salary?
   B. Two hundred fifty-five dollars a week.

A. Two hundred fifty-five dollars?
B. Yes. That's right.

5. A. What are the hours?
   B. Nine o'clock to five thirty.

A. Nine to five thirty?
B. Yes. That's right.

6. A. What are the hours?
   B. Seven thirty to three thirty.

A. Seven thirty to three thirty?
B. Yes. That's right.

7. A. What are the hours?
   B. Ten o'clock to two o'clock.

A. Ten to two?
B. Yes. That's right.

8. A. What are the hours?
   B. Six o'clock to nine o'clock.

A. Six to nine?
B. Yes. That's right.

Page 108

Listen and draw an X under the correct picture.

1. A. Excuse me. Can I eat here?
   B. Eat? No. There's the sign.

2. A. Excuse me. Can I smoke here?
   B. Smoke? No. There's the sign.

3. A. Can I park here?
   B. Park? No. There's the sign.

4. A. Can I fish here?
   B. Fish? No. There's the sign.

5. A. Can I eat here?
   B. Eat? No. There's the sign.

6. A. Can I swim here?
   B. Swim? No. There's the sign.

Page 109

Listen and circle.

1. Can I fish here?

2. Can I eat here?

3. Can I swim here?

4. Can I park here?

5. Can I smoke here?

6. Can I fish here?

Page 111

Listen and circle.

1. A. Excuse me. Where's the telephone?

B. It's right over there. Do you see the sign "Phones?"

2. A. Excuse me. Where's the parking lot?
   B. It's right over there. Do you see the sign "Parking?"

3. A. Excuse me. Where's the ladies' room?
   B. It's right over there. Do you see the sign "Rest Rooms?"

4. A. Excuse me. Where's the cafeteria?
   B. It's right over there. Do you see the sign "Lunch Room?"

5. Excuse me. Where's the parking lot?

6. Excuse me. Where's the lunch room?

7. Excuse me. Where's the men's room?

Page 115

Listen and circle.

1. A. Do you want to do something on Friday?
   B. I can't. I have to go to the airport.

2. A. Do you want to do something on Monday?
   B. I can't. I have to go to the laundromat.

3. A. Do you want to do something on Tuesday?
   B. I can't. I have to go to the clinic.

4. A. Do you want to do something on Saturday?
   B. I can't. I have to go to the supermarket.

5. A. Do you want to do something on Sunday?
   B. On Sunday? I can't. I have to go to the airport.

6. A. Do you want to do something on Saturday?
   B. On Saturday? I can't. I have to go to the clinic.

7. A. Do you want to do something on Friday?
   B. On Friday? I can't. I have to go to the laundromat.

8. A. Do you want to do something on Thursday?
   B. On Thursday? I can't. I have to go to the supermarket.

Page 115

Listen and write on the calendar.

1. A. Do you want to do something on Monday?
   B. On Monday? I can't. I have to go to the laundromat.

2. A. Do you want to do something on Friday?
   B. On Friday? I can't. I have to go to the hospital.

3. A. Do you want to do something on Saturday?
   B. On Saturday? I can't. I have to go to the supermarket.

4. A. Do you want to do something on Wednesday?
   B. On Wednesday? I can't. I have to go to the clinic.

5. A. Do you want to do something on Sunday?
   B. On Sunday? I can't. I have to go to the airport.

Page 118

Listen and write an X under the correct sign.

1. A. The bank is open from eight thirty to three thirty.
   B. Eight thirty to three thirty?
   A. Yes. That's right.

2. A. The clinic is open from seven fifteen to five forty-five.
   B. From seven fifteen to five forty-five?
   A. Yes. That's right.

3. A. The post office is open from eight fifteen to four forty-five.
   B. From eight fifteen to four forty-five?
   A. Yes. That's right.

4. A. The supermarket is open Monday through Friday from eight to six.
   B. Monday through Friday from eight to six?
   A. Yes. That's right.

Page 119

Listen and write the time.

1. A. What time is it?
   B. It's one thirty.
   A. Oh! I've got to get to the clinic!

2. A. What time is it?
   B. It's five fifteen.
   A. Oh! I've got to get to the airport!

3. A. What time is it?
   B. It's twelve forty-five.
   A. Oh! I've got to get to the hospital!

4. A. What time is it?
   B. It's nine thirty.
   A. Oh! I've got to get to class!

5. A. What time is it?
   B. It's three fifteen.
   A. Oh! I've got to get to the post office!

6. A. What time is it?
   B. It's eleven forty-five.
   A. Oh! I've got to get to the bank!

A B C D E F G H I

J K L M N O P Q R

S T U V W X Y Z

a b c d e f g h i

j k l m n o p q r

s t u v w x y z

1 2 3 4 5 6 7 8 9 10